Fun with the Family™ New Mexico

Praise for the *Fun with the Family*™ series

"Enables parents to turn family travel into an exploration."
—Alexandra Kennedy, Editor, *Family Fun*

"Bound to lead you and your kids to fun-filled days,
those times that help compose the
memories of childhood."
—Dorothy Jordon, *Family Travel Times*

Help Us Keep This Guide Up to Date

Every effort has been made by the authors and editors to make this guide as accurate and useful as possible. However, many changes can occur after a guide is published—establishments close, phone numbers change, hiking trails are rerouted, facilities come under new management, etc.

We would love to hear from you concerning your experiences with this guide and how you feel it could be improved and be kept up to date. While we may not be able to respond to all comments and suggestions, we'll take them to heart, and we'll make certain to share them with the authors. Please send your comments and suggestions to the following address:

The Globe Pequot Press
Reader Response/Editorial Department
P.O. Box 480
Guilford, CT 06437

Or you may e-mail us at: editorial@GlobePequot.com

Thanks for your input, and happy travels!

INSIDERS' GUIDE®

FUN WITH THE FAMILY™ SERIES

fun WITH the Family™

NEW MEXICO

HUNDREDS OF IDEAS FOR DAY TRIPS WITH THE KIDS

KATE WINSLOW AND JULIA WARD

FOURTH EDITION

INSIDERS' GUIDE®

GUILFORD, CONNECTICUT
AN IMPRINT OF THE GLOBE PEQUOT PRESS

The prices, rates, and hours listed in this guidebook
were confirmed at press time. We recommend, however, that you call establishments to obtain current
information before traveling.

To buy books in quantity for corporate use
or incentives, call **(800) 962–0973, ext. 4551,**
or e-mail **premiums@GlobePequot.com.**

INSIDERS' GUIDE®

Text design by Nancy Freeborn and Linda Loiewski
Maps by Rusty Nelson © The Globe Pequot Press
Spot photography throughout © Photodisc

ISSN 1545-7621
ISBN 0-7627-3494-9

Manufactured in the United States of America
Fourth Edition/First Printing

For CJ, Ethan, Shae, Kendall, and Tracy—
thank you for making my first memories of New Mexico so precious.

NEW MEXICO

Contents

Introduction

New Mexico is called the Land of Enchantment; it is a place like no other in the world, physically and historically. Billy the Kid lived in Silver City, and Doc Holliday had a saloon in Las Vegas. World War II scientists built the atomic bomb in Los Alamos and tested it at Trinity Site. New Mexico has Carlsbad Caverns, pueblos, a large chunk of the Navajo Reservation, some exciting skiing spots, even scuba diving.

As you travel through the state, you can't help but notice how sparsely populated it is. Catron County in the southwestern part of the state, for example, is as large as Connecticut, with only eleven small towns spread out through its expanses. This is still the frontier but all the more interesting because of it. Your kids will be amazed at the wildlife, vast deserts, and forests they'll rarely see anywhere else.

To make your trip easier, we've divided the state into six regions: Northeast, Northwest, Southeast, Southwest, North Central, and Central. There are maps to each section, with annual community events and where to stay and eat noted at the end of each entry, a general index, and a glossary of terms that may be unfamiliar.

A note about where to stay and where to eat: Except for the central corridor of Taos, Santa Fe, and Albuquerque, other segments of the state have modest, small towns with one or two main streets and all of the hotels and restaurants clustered along these stretches. For restaurants, you will find mostly cafes and diners serving local Southwestern dishes (see glossary). Hotels and motels, for the most part, are unpretentious but clean, and they always welcome families. If you remember that these are frontier towns where the businesses catering to tourists are usually family-owned, you can arrange your traveling schedule to stop early for accommodations and meals.

Visiting the Pueblos and Reservations

Visiting Native American territory can be interesting and exciting, but there's a certain protocol to follow. You will have a better time (and so will residents) if you know beforehand what is expected of visitors.

Pueblos and reservations have strict regulations about where visitors can and can't go. Usually there is a sign at the entrance making such stipulations clear. While each pueblo operates under its own government and makes its own rules for visitors, the pueblos can be divided into those that are considered "progressive" and those that are "traditional." Broadly, progressive pueblos are those that support themselves more directly from the tourist industry and take the opportunity to open themselves up to the public, while those that are traditional are more self-contained, farming communities and may only be open to visitors on some feast days.

Photography may be a sensitive issue for both types of pueblos and the reservations you may visit. Some do not permit it at all, while others request a fee for camera use. These fees can range from $5.00 to $30.00. Most definitely any pictures that are taken must be only for private use.

When you and your family attend ceremonial dances, it is important to remember that these are sacred rituals, not just performances. It is like being at church, so quiet and respectful attention is requested. There are times between dances when the participants are resting or praying, so these times may be better for talking to those who are not participating or taking a break, too. Applauding is not advised, just so you know, and questions should be directed to the visitor's area, not the pueblo members (unless you are invited to do so). On feast days, pueblo members sometimes will invite outsiders to share a meal with them in their home. If you are invited, it is courteous to accept if you can, then eat quietly and quickly, leaving without lingering too long, since those who are doing the inviting will be serving many guests during the day.

What else? Generally, no pets are allowed (and no alcohol, weapons, or drugs, please). It's a good idea to call the pueblo or reservation before you visit to learn what its particular policies are.

General Safety Tips
Weather

Let's face it, New Mexico is unpredictable in terms of weather, and to try to calculate what you will need is futile. Prepare for the worst and hope for the best. No matter what the season, layer, layer, layer and make sure that one of the layers is waterproof. Even in the relatively temperate summertime, things can begin sunny and warm, then quickly turn ugly (and vice versa). Expect a shower or full-fledged thunderstorm once a day during the afternoon in the summer months. It will be brief and, like a good cry, can refresh the atmosphere and your mood. Sunscreen is important because of the increased ultraviolet light exposure at high altitudes. The altitudes by themselves can affect how you feel, too. You may feel sluggish or hit a "wall" when normal exertion at home would leave you unaffected. Alcohol hits you harder, too. The good thing is that water boils at 198°F at 7,000 feet, which has been calculated as the perfect temperature for making coffee. Take it easy, and be sure to drink plenty of water—dehydration at these altitudes can lead to severe headaches.

Desert and Mountain

You will find lots of opportunity to experience both in New Mexico. In the desert there are sometimes great expanses with no civilization for 50 to 60 miles, so take these conditions seriously. If your car breaks down, you may have to wait quite a while for help. It is important to carry enough water for everyone traveling (about one gallon per person per day). A blanket or two and a stash of good snacks are advised, in addition to a first aid kit. As I said, the weather can change drastically and becomes more pronounced as you climb. In the mountains, every 1,000 feet up is equivalent to traveling 300 miles farther north. It is assumed that if you want to camp, you already know how, or how to find out. We can tell you about some beautiful spots, but remember that outdoors in New Mexico really means OUTDOORS, so be sure you plan for what you will need at all times: more food, more water, more clothes. (Three notes on hot springs: Expect some nudity [feel free to join in—*au naturel*, of course]; you probably shouldn't go in if you're pregnant, but check with your doctor; and watch out for poison ivy in the area.)

Nastiness

New Mexico is beautiful, but the great outdoors can pose some problems. Besides the glorious sunsets, spectacular vistas, and intoxicating scents of juniper and sage, there are rattlesnakes, scorpions, two kinds of poisonous spiders, and, oh yes, some fleas that carry the plague.

Your experience with these creatures will be limited, however, if you follow some common sense. Most are shy and retiring types that become aggressive only when they feel threatened or hang out where you really shouldn't be anyway. So don't sleep in fields, make a little noise when you walk, and watch where you're walking. No sandals in dark places, please. If you bring pets with you, deflea them when you get home, and don't touch dead animals (they can harbor the fleas that carry the plague). Spring and autumn, when the juniper and chamisa bloom, are the prime allergy seasons in New Mexico. If you or any family members are allergy prone, pack some extra medicine and tissues for your trip.

The real danger, though, is that you won't expose yourself and your family to all that New Mexico can share with you.

Traveling with Children

Throughout the book, you will see icons that should help you quickly determine what might be fun for your family, in addition to a suggested age range. When attractions in the book indicate "all ages," it is because we think that there is probably something of interest for everyone. "Ages 10 to 12" means that those places require either surer footing or a deeper interest (or attention) than a younger child may have. We assume that you know who your children are and what they like, so you must determine whether a particular museum or art gallery is suited for them. Beyond that, if you haven't yet taken an extensive trip together, think practically: Plan ahead (see below) and take lots of breaks (don't forget some for you, too). Inform your children of what to expect, then let the kids help you plan your day or let them lead now and again.

Planning Ahead

First, there is only one area code for the entire state: 505. That tells you a lot about the population, or lack of it.

We included a Fast Facts list at the beginning of the book as a guide to sources that can answer any questions you may have. Just scan it so you know what's there. A particularly good Web site is the New Mexico Public Lands Information Center (PLIC) site (www.publiclands.org). Instead of contacting the National Parks Service, the Forest Service, the Bureau of Land Management, etc., you can contact the PLIC, a private, nonprofit organization that can meet all of your outdoor needs. It even supplies fishing and gaming licenses. For smaller towns and hamlets that can't support their own visitor bureaus, contact the New Mexico Department of Tourism.

With these precautions in mind, enjoy the cowboys and Indians, the mesas and sunsets, the fishing and hiking, the volcanoes and dinosaurs. A visit to New Mexico is guaranteed to be a fascinating, unforgettable encounter with the Land of Enchantment.

Lodging and Restaurant Rates

In the Where to Eat and Where to Stay sections, dollar signs indicate general price ranges:

New Mexico FastFacts

- **Bureau of Land Management**
  (505) 438–7840
  www.nm.blm.gov

- **Eight Northern Indian Pueblos Council Tourism Department**
  (505) 747–0700

- **Indian Pueblo Cultural Center**
  2401 Twelfth Street NW
  Albuquerque, NM 87104
  (505) 843–7270 or
  (800) 766–4405
  www.indianpueblo.org

- **Navajo Nation Tourism**
  (928) 871–6436
  www.discovernavaho.com

- **New Mexico Bed and Breakfast Association**
  (800) 661–6649
  www.nmbba.org

- **New Mexico Department of Game and Fish**
  1 Wildlife Lane
  Santa Fe, NM 87505
  (505) 476–8000 or
  (800) 862–9310
  www.wildlife.state.nm.us

Rates for Lodging

Lodging prices reflect the cost of one hotel room with two double beds.

$	$50 and under
$$	$51 to $100
$$$	$101 and up

Rates for Restaurants

Restaurant rates are for an average entree.

$	$8.00 and under
$$	$9.00 to $14.00
$$$	$15.00 and up

- New Mexico Department of Tourism
  491 Old Santa Fe Trail
  Santa Fe, NM 87503
  (505) 827–7400 or
  (800) 733–6396
  www.newmexico.org

- New Mexico Guides Organization
  P.O. Box 1601
  Santa Fe, NM 87504
  (505) 988–8022
  www.nmgo.com

- New Mexico Lodging Association
  (505) 983–4554
  www.nmlodging.org

- New Mexico Public Lands Information Center
  1474 Rodeo Road
  Santa Fe, NM 87505
  (505) 438–7542 or
  (877) 276–9404
  www.publiclands.org

- New Mexico Road Conditions
  8:00 A.M.–5:00 P.M. weekdays, in-state only
  (800) 432–4269

- New Mexico Rodeo Association
  (505) 280–7891
  nmrodeo.org

- New Mexico State Parks
  1220 South St. Francis Drive
  Santa Fe, NM 87505
  (888) 667–2757
  www.nmparks.com

- Professional Rodeo Cowboys Association
  (719) 593–8840 (for seasonal listing of rodeos)

- Publication: Buying Native American Arts and Crafts
  Office of the Attorney General
  P.O. Box 1508
  Santa Fe, NM 87504–1508
  (505) 827–6000

- Ski New Mexico and New Mexico Ski Conditions
  (505) 982–5300 or
  (800) 755–7669
  www.skinewmexico.com

- USDA Forest Service
  (505) 829–3535
  www.fs.fed.us

Attractions Key

The following is a key to the icons found throughout the text.

SWIMMING		FOOD	
BOATING / BOAT TOUR		LODGING	
HISTORIC SITE		CAMPING	
HIKING / WALKING		MUSEUMS	
FISHING		PERFORMING ARTS	
BIKING		SPORTS/ATHLETICS	
AMUSEMENT PARK		PICNICKING	
HORSEBACK RIDING		PLAYGROUND	
SKIING/WINTER SPORTS		SHOPPING	
PARK		PLANTS/GARDENS/NATURE TRAILS	
ANIMAL VIEWING		FARMS	

Central New Mexico

Yes, Central New Mexico is dominated now by the sprawling city of Albuquerque, but the Rio Grande has been a quiet, omnipresent force in this valley for thousands of years; its sustained influence is really the key to life in the area. Take time to explore its beauty while you enjoy the rich heritage of Albuquerque. From the volcanic red rocks and calderas of the Jémez Mountains to the well-preserved and stirring pueblo ruins of Gran Quivira, this area offers a perfect mix of desert, mountain, and river intermingled with the best of city life (both past and present).

Albuquerque

Interstate 25 and Interstate 40.

The largest city in New Mexico, Albuquerque is the business pulse of the state as well. All major manufacturing is centered here, as is the Sunport International Airport, the University of New Mexico, Kirtland Air Force Base, and the farm team for the Los Angeles Dodgers. But don't let the high-rises and vast malls distract you from the historic Old Town, with its charming adobe buildings. The city also has a museum of natural history with dinosaurs for the kids to study at close range. The delightful Rio Grande Zoo, packed with an unbelievable array of animals, rivals some of the best in the country, and the beautiful Albuquerque Aquarium lets you observe sharks, eels, and a coral reef. The Indian Pueblo Cultural Center welcomes all children interested in the history of Native Americans, from the Anasazi to present-day pueblo dwellers. And there are still more pueblos for your children to visit, including the San Felipe and Santo Domingo Pueblos. For kids who love mountains and adventures, the Tramway takes them up into the sky and over the highest mountains in Albuquerque. The area also features some wonderful Anasazi petroglyphs and the Rattlesnake Museum.

Albuquerque was founded in 1706 when a land grant was given to a group of families by King Felipe V of Spain. This, of course, was many years after Coronado passed through the area in 1540, when there were many thousands of Pueblo Indians living alongside each other and a wilder, grander Rio Grande. The settlement was named "Alburquerque,"

CENTRAL

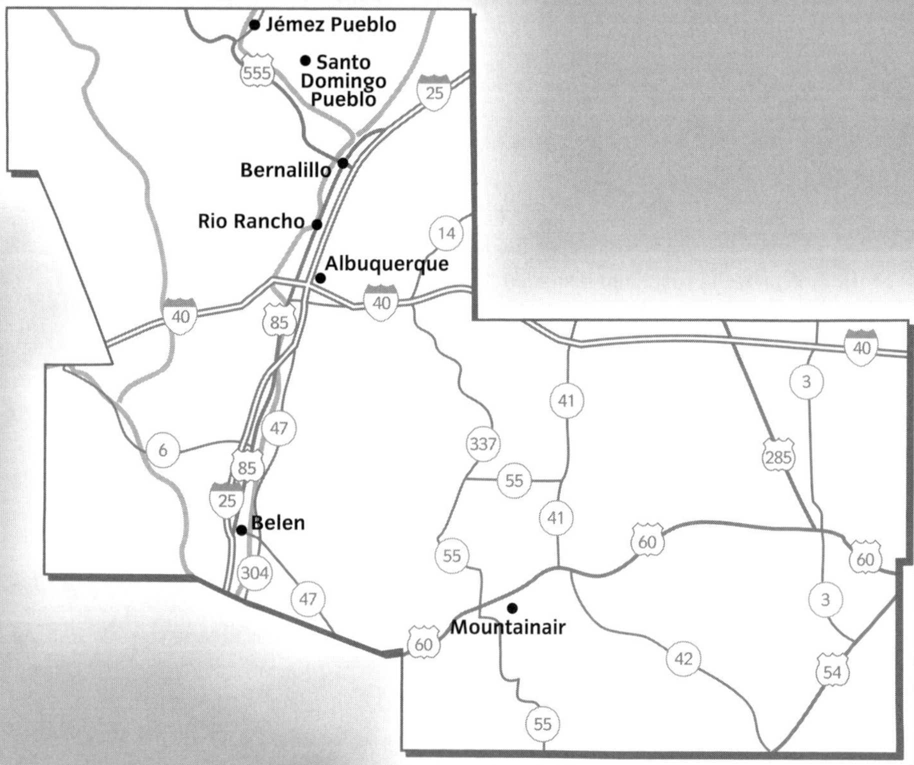

Jémez Pueblo

Santo Domingo Pueblo

555

25

Bernalillo

Rio Rancho

14

Albuquerque

40

40

85

3

40

41

6

47

337

285

85

55

25

41

60

Belen

55

60

304

3

47

60

Mountainair

42

54

55

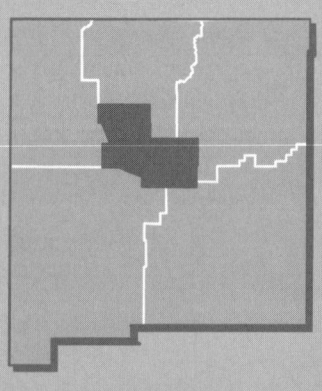

after the viceroy of New Spain. When the Americans assumed New Mexico as a territory, they dropped the first *r*. Albuquerque soon grew as the first major stop on the Chihuahua Trail, the branch of the Santa Fe Trail that extended from Santa Fe to Mexico. It also helped that it was on the main waterway of the Southwest. After the railroad came, Albuquerque became a military base. The University of New Mexico became another central attraction when it was established in 1889. The city was again popular in the early twentieth century when people flocked to the sanatoriums here to recuperate from tuberculosis.

Old Town (all ages)

I–25 to I–40 west. Take Rio Grande Boulevard exit and go east, following the signs. Information Center is at 305 Romero Street.

Note: At the height of the summer tourist season, parking will be a challenge. Prepare for the possibility that you and the kids will have to park and walk.

As with every New Mexican town or city, the plaza is the focus of community life. Albuquerque's a great place to stroll and take in a little history. The pretty common is full of shops, restaurants, and galleries. The cannons at the center are replicas of the original Civil War weapons that the withdrawing Confederate troops buried behind the church (the originals are in the Albuquerque Museum). The bronze equestrian statue at the corner of Mountain and Rio Grande represents Don Francisco Cuervo y Valdes, who founded *la villa de Alburquerque* in 1706.

San Felipe Neri Church (ages 10 to 12)

San Felipe Neri dominates the plaza and has been witness to all the postcolonial happenings ever since it was built in 1792 (a second time, after the original parish church, built in 1706, was destroyed in a flood in 1791). It is a charming adobe building open to the public. San Felipe is Albuquerque's patron saint. Behind the church building, now housing several art galleries, is the former convent, where the locally famous Sister of

Nature Trails **in Town**

There are three trails at the foothills of the Sandias (northeast quadrant of the city) that are short, comfortable, and let you take a break from the modern world. The first one, **Embudo,** is at the end of Indian School Road. The second, **Embudito,** is farther north, all the way out just after Montgomery and Camino de la Sierra come together. Still farther north is the **Pino** at **Gallegos Park,** off the Tramway between Paseo Norte to the north and Academy to the south. An extension of this trail goes up to Sandia Peak.

Charity Blandina Segale lived. In the early days of Albuquerque, this amazing woman built schools, ministered to settlers, even prevented Billy the Kid from shooting all the doctors in town—as he had promised to do.

American International Rattlesnake Museum (all ages)

202 San Felipe NW; (505) 242–6569; www.rattlesnakes.com. Open Monday through Saturday 10:00 A.M. to 6:00 P.M., Sunday noon to 5:00 P.M. Admission: $2.50 for adults, $2.00 for seniors, $1.50 for children 12 and under.

On the southeast corner of the plaza is the Rattlesnake Museum, which opened in 1990. Bob Myers, the owner, is on the spot daily to take you through the exhibit and talk about his favorite subject: rattlesnakes. This is a small, unpretentious exhibit, but that's all to the better. You and the children can take your time, talk to Bob, and enjoy the whole experience in a very personal and relaxed atmosphere, learning about conservation and preservation through education. The owner has gone to the trouble of providing informative signs for both adults and children. The collection has the largest accumulation of rattlesnake species in the world. If you and your children are used to the scary rattlers you see in cowboy movies, this collection will open your eyes. The kids will be entranced by the various colors and sizes of these creatures.

Turquoise Museum (all ages)

2107 Central NW; (505) 247–8650. Open weekdays 9:30 A.M. to 4:00 P.M., Saturday until 3:00 P.M. Admission: $4.00 for adults, $3.00 for seniors and children 7–18.

On the other side of the plaza is another tiny but informative showplace tucked away in a storefront. This, too, is a down-home experience for the kids. The Lowry-Zachary family owns the Turquoise Museum and is there to talk with you and take you through the exhibit. There's a replica of a mine tunnel and an interesting display of rare and valuable turquoise in a no-fuss, utilitarian setting. While the kids enjoy the tunnel, you can get valu-

Shopping

Here are some shops to explore:

- **Hello Dollie Doll Shoppe.** 324 San Felipe NW, C-3; (505) 247–3990
- **Old Town Basket and Rug Shop.** 301 Romero NW; (505) 842–8022
- **Rocky Mountain Chocolate Factory.** 303 Romero NW; (505) 842–8883
- **Satellite.** 3513 Central NE; (505) 256–0345. Great coffee shop with an array of funky toys, gifts, and books.

Balloon **Rides**

- **Rainbow Ryders.** 10305 Nita Place NE; (505) 823–1111 or (800) 725–2477; www.rainbowryders.com.
- **Albuquerque Sweet Escape Balloon Rides.** 216 Dogwood Trail SE, Rio Rancho; (505) 891–7634 or (800) 385–4453.

able information about what to look for before you buy a piece of jewelry. Ask to see the unique Larder Blue County, Nevada turquoise. Only 108 pounds of this type have ever been extracted. There is also a gift shop.

Albuquerque Museum of Art and History (ages 10 to 12) 🏛

2000 Mountain Road; (505) 243–7255. Open Tuesday through Sunday 9:00 A.M. to 5:00 P.M. Admission: $4.00 for adults, $2.00 for seniors, $1.00 for children 4–12.

A block from the plaza, you and the kids can walk through the outdoor sculpture garden, which is full of accessible works of art that the children can even play on. Indoors, look for the originals of those Civil War cannons that you may have seen at the plaza. Exhibits are nicely presented, and there are frequent family classes and programs.

New Mexico Museum of Natural History and Science (all ages) 🏛

1801 Mountain Road NW; (505) 841–2800. Open daily from 9:00 A.M. to 5:00 P.M. Museum admission: $5.00 for adults, $4.00 for seniors, $2.00 for children 3–12. Theater admission: $6.00 for adults, $5.00 for seniors, $3.00 for children 3–12.

There are wonderful bronze statues of some glorious dinosaurs outside. Inside, the children can enjoy a look at some of the most enormous dinosaur bones they'll ever see, as

Amusement **Parks**

- **The Beach Waterpark.** 1600 Desert Surf Loop (near I–25 and Montgomery); (505) 345–6066. A lazy "river," a kiddie pool, seven slides, and a wave pool.
- **Cliff's Amusement Park.** 4800 Osuna NE; (505) 881–9373; www.cliffs.net. A traditional amusement park with more than twenty rides to amuse all ages. Picnic facilities, too.
- **Hinkle Family Fun Center.** 12931 Indian School NE; (505) 299–3100. Families can enjoy laser tag, bumper boats, a mini go-kart racetrack, and miniature golf.

well as skeletons of various ancient species in attractively arranged dioramas. You can explore an ice cave, go "inside" a live volcano, or ride the Evolator 70 million years back to the age of dinosaurs. There are permanent and changing exhibits that focus on biology, geology, zoology, and paleontology. There's even a jungle room full of plants of a size you could only imagine. Be sure to take the kids to the **Dynamax** theater, a wraparound large-format cinema with changing film selections. Recent offerings have been about beavers, wild plants of the pueblos, the flora of the Southwest, and Mayan culture. Shows run daily every hour on the hour from 10:00 A.M. to 5:00 P.M.

Explora! Science Center and the Children's Museum of Albuquerque (all ages)

800 Rio Grande Boulevard NW; (505) 224–8300; www.explora.mus.nm.us. Open Monday through Saturday 10:00 A.M. to 6:00 P.M., Sunday noon to 6:00 P.M. Admission: $7.00 for adults, $5.00 for seniors, $3.00 for children 1–11.

You'll definitely want to take the kids to this museum, which is attached to the Sheraton Old Town. This is a private, nonprofit museum for the whole family. There's a bubble-blowing room where the kids can blow bubbles from wands as big as watermelons or as small as peas. There's also a Victorian frontier village set up with a home (complete with an old-fashioned stove), a cantina, a store, and a bank. The kids can play in these areas until you beg them to come out. Every season, the central part of the museum has a changing exhibit. Recent exhibits have been a gas station and a racecar. There's also a Computer Discovery Lab. It's all great fun for everyone. The Explora! is a hands-on interactive science center, inviting your kids to play with and learn about the wonders of science and technology. There are thirty-five different exhibits to play with, mostly dealing with electricity and sound. Guides are there to help and explain. The kids won't want to leave.

Rio Grande Nature Center State Park (all ages)

2901 Candelaria NW; (505) 344–7240; www.frgnc.org. Open daily from 10:00 A.M. to 5:00 P.M. Admission: $1.00 for adults, 50 cents for children under 17.

This is a marvelous natural environment that edges along the Rio Grande in the heart of the city. There's plenty of **free** parking, too. With twenty-one different self-guided interpretive exhibits to follow, you and your family will gain wonderful insights into the importance of this historical river. One of the delights of the Nature Center is the entrance to the main visitor building through what looks like a huge pipe. Be sure you go into the glass-walled library. From there your kids can see a water inlet fringed with woodlands (known as a bosque) and the hundreds of birds and types of wildlife that use this area. There are weekend programs for children and adults and a children's hands-on resource room.

Rio Grande Zoo (all ages)

903 Tenth Street (from I-25, take Lead Avenue for approximately a mile, then turn left on Tenth Street); (505) 764–6200. Open daily from 9:00 A.M. to 5:00 P.M. Admission: $7.00 for adults, $3.00 for seniors and children under 12.

This part of the Albuquerque Biological Park is another "must-see" experience for the whole family. Plan to spend the day here. There are snack bars throughout the area if you want to take a break. There are also strollers and wheelchairs for rent. The aquarium and botanic garden are also part of this complex (see below).

As you and your family walk through this beautifully landscaped setting, you'll get to watch flamingos, elephants, polar bears, cheetahs, white Bengal tigers, monkeys, and giraffes, to name a few of the 1,200 animals, birds, and reptiles on view. There's a sea world of seals and sea lions; feeding times are posted so the kids can see what happens during meals. This is a wonderland for both you and the kids that you shouldn't miss even if you come from a large city with its own zoo.

Note: The zoo doesn't allow pets on the grounds—even assistance animals. Guided tours are available for the disabled on request.

Albuquerque Aquarium and Rio Grande Botanic Garden (all ages)
2601 Central Avenue NW; (505) 764–6200. Open daily 9:00 A.M. to 5:00 P.M. Admission: $7.00 for adults, $3.00 for children under 12.

One of the exhibits in the aquarium shows what happens as a drop of water flows from the Rio Grande to the Gulf of Mexico. In this Albuquerque Biological Park facility, you'll also find an impressive shark tank (you feel as if you are in the water with them), a walkway through an eel cave, an open artificial coral reef, and many other examples of ecosystems that occur underwater. The botanic garden showcases the diversity of the natural environments found in the Mediterranean and Southwest climates.

National Atomic Museum (ages 10 to 12)
1905 Mountain Road NW; (505) 245–2137; www.atomicmuseum.com. Open daily from 9:00 A.M. to 5:00 P.M. Admission: $4.00 for adults, $3.00 for children 7–18 and seniors 55 and older.

Here your kids will get to examine replicas of Little Boy and Fat Man—the casings used to drop the atomic bombs on Hiroshima and Nagasaki, Japan. Check out the B-52 bomber and F-105D fighter plane, as well as the many models of nuclear-powered submarines and a 280 mm cannon capable of propelling a 600-pound shell 20 miles. This is not necessarily a place to get an unbiased view of nuclear testing or to untangle the ambiguity of progress in the development of atomic energy, but you're sure to come out more informed about nuclear science than when you went in.

Indian Pueblo Cultural Center (all ages)
2401 Twelfth Street NW; (505) 843–7270; www.indianpueblo.com. Open daily 9:00 A.M. to 5:30 P.M. Children's museum open by appointment. Restaurant open 8:00 A.M. to 3:00 P.M. Admission: $4.00 for adults, $3.00 for seniors, $1.00 for students and children 4–17; under 4 admitted free.

This is a great opportunity for you and your family to experience the art and history of Native American culture. The center is owned and operated by the nineteen pueblo tribes of northern New Mexico and is a treasure trove of Native American history. Every weekend (from mid-April to mid-October) there are tribal dance performances (check times, but

Professional Sports

- **Albuquerque Isotopes** (baseball) (505) 924–2255; www.albuquerquebaseball.com. The Triple-A farm team of the Florida Marlins plays in a brand-new stadium.
- **New Mexico Scorpions** (hockey) Tingley Coliseum; (505) 881–7825; www.scorpionshockey.com.

usually they're at 11:00 A.M. and 2:00 P.M.). All through the year cultural presentations are offered, including arts and crafts workshops, a Pueblo Harvest, and a Father's Day Multicultural Festival. The center has its own restaurant featuring tasty Native American dishes. There are also wraparound gift shops where you can be sure that profits from the sales go both to the artists and to the support of this repository of Indian culture and history. The hands-on children's museum on the grounds is a cozy adobe cottage where the kids can examine pottery, blankets, and other items made by Native Americans.

Maxwell Museum of Anthropology (ages 10 to 12)

On the campus of the University of New Mexico. Take I–25 to Martin Luther King Boulevard; (505) 277–4404 or (505) 277–4405; www.unm.edu/~maxwell. Open Tuesday through Friday 9:00 A.M. to 4:00 P.M., Saturday 10:00 A.M. to 4:00 P.M. Admission: by donation. Free parking.

The Maxwell Museum is good for explorations into the history of humankind. Founded in 1932, it was the first public museum in Albuquerque. Your kids will especially enjoy the Ancestors Exhibit, which takes them through four million years of human development, with reconstructed cave settings full of Ice Age drawings and sculptures. Other displays include artifacts from New Guinea, Pakistan, Indonesia, and Africa.

Nob Hill Area (ages 10 to 12)

Central Avenue and Carlisle Boulevard (part of Route 66).

In 1926 Route 66 was recognized as a major thoroughfare linking Chicago and Los Angeles. Central Avenue is the bit of it that runs through Albuquerque. It is no longer the main traffic artery, but it runs through a historic neighborhood that may appeal to families with older children. Innumerable buildings have that 1950s look. The area also borders the University of New Mexico, and the shops around it echo its vitality. There are lots of bookstores, coffee shops, restaurants, and boutiques lining Central Avenue.

Child Care in Albuquerque

Professional Nannies of New Mexico. (505) 299–6181. In-room care for visitors.

Sandia Peak Tramway (all ages)

Tramway Boulevard off I–25, or take I–40 to exit 167, then follow the signs; (505) 856–7325 or (505) 856–1532; www.sandiapeak.com. Open daily 9:00 A.M. to 9:00 P.M. Admission: $15 for adults, $12 for seniors, and $10 for children 5–12; under 5 **free.**

The world's largest aerial tramway offers a glorious view of the Sandia Mountains and Albuquerque and over the Domingo Baca Canyon. As you glide the 10,000 feet to the top of Sandia Peak, you and the kids will gasp at the vistas. Of the 24 miles of trails for hiking or biking, some can be accessed at the base and the rest from the top. *Be warned:* This is not a Sunday stroll. You'll be 10,000 feet up, and the weather changes rapidly. The trails can be arduous, too. Use caution, take snacks and water, and dress appropriately for high mountain climbing. Once you get to the top there's a visitor center and two places to eat. There are also spectacular night rides. It is worth taking the kids up in the evening to see the twinkling lights of the city below. **Sandiago's Mexican Grill** (505–856–6692) is located at the base of the mountain, or you can eat at the **High Finance Restaurant** (505–243–9742) at the peak. There are dinner/ride specials with advance reservations.

Sandia Crest (all ages)

I–40 east to exit 175 (Highway 14), go north and get off at the Sandia Crest Highway (exit 536); (505) 243–0605. Trail is **free** and open to the public from sunrise to sunset.

The trip up is a longish, meandering ride to 10,678 feet and the peak. There are tremendous views of modern Albuquerque, as well as a layout showing Albuquerque of fifty years ago. Your kids will enjoy looking out at the sprawling city, then glancing down at the

Swimming (Summer Only)

- **Highland Pool,** corner of San Mateo and Zuni; (505) 256–2096
- **Los Altos Pool,** 10100 Lomas NE; (505) 291–6290
- **Sunport Pool,** 2033 Columbia SE; (505) 848–1398
- **Valley Pool,** 1505 Candelaria NW; (505) 761–4086

Annual Community Events

LAST WEEKEND OF APRIL

Gathering of Nations. UNM Arena; (505) 836–2810; www.gatheringof
nations.com. Described as the Native American State Fair, most of New Mexico's pueblos and tribes are represented in a week full of powwows, dances,
and indigenous food offerings.

JUNE AND JULY (SATURDAYS)

Summerfest. Downtown; (505) 768–3483. Enjoy a multievent celebration of
cultural diversity.

LATE JUNE

New Mexico Arts and Crafts Fair. State Fairgrounds; (505) 884–9043. More
than 200 artists from all over New Mexico come to this juried art show. Concerts and good food, too.

FOURTH OF JULY

Fourth of July Fireworks. At the stadium (off Gibson); (505) 842–9918.
Albuquerque takes the Fourth of July seriously!

SEPTEMBER

New Mexico State Fair. State Fairgrounds (on Louisiana between Lomas and
Central); (505) 265–1791; www.NMStateFair.com. Starts Friday after Labor Day.
This is the eighth-largest state fair in the nation. Choose from quarterhorse and
thoroughbred racing, lots of arts and crafts, lots of wonderful music and food,
amusement park rides, reconstructed Indian, Spanish, and frontier villages, livestock shows, and general good-natured mayhem for seventeen days.

EARLY OCTOBER

Albuquerque International Balloon Fiesta. (505) 821–1000; www.aibf.org.
Should you plan to visit the city in early October, you and your family will be
just in time to participate in this major event, with more than 600 balloons of
all shapes and sizes. The mass ascensions at sunrise will have your children
simply amazed as hundreds of vividly colored hot-air balloons lift up into the
dawn sky. One of the most delightful events during this weeklong fiesta is
the Special Shapes Mass Ascent. Balloons in the shape of a telephone, a
hamburger, a hot dog, and a mammoth polar bear float aloft like cotton
candy. There is also the Balloon-Glow, on some designated evenings, when

the balloons remain on the ground, but are inflated and are lit. *Note:* The fiesta can be noisy and crowded, and if you have small, shy children who will be more unnerved than entertained, it may be enough for them to see the ascent from I–25 early in the morning, watching the balloons from the quiet of the car.

layout and marveling at the difference. There is a ¼-mile self-guided tour along a path leading out from the summit gift/snack bar. Again, if you and your family go out, wear proper shoes and dress in layers because the weather can be chilly, even in the summer. This is not a place for strollers or baby backpacks as the trail, while paved, is uneven in spots.

Tinkertown Museum (all ages)
125 Sandia Crest Road. Take I–40 east to exit 175 (Highway 14), and go north, turning left at the Sandia Crest Highway (exit 536); the museum is on the left about a ¼-mile up; (505) 281–5233; www.tinkertown.com. Open April through October, 9:00 A.M. to 6:00 P.M. Admission: $3.00 for those 17 and older, $1.00 for children 4–16.

For an unforgettably offbeat experience, take your kids to the Tinkertown Museum. The brainchild of Ross and Carla Ward, this is a one-of-a-kind place. The walls of the exhibits are composed of bottles cemented together—40,000 of them! The museum is decorated with old license plates and memorabilia (my son and I got **free** admission when I

donated two 1920 New York plates). Their motto is "We did all this while you were watching television," and what they did was to hand-carve and animate a miniature town and circus. It is quite a sight to see.

Petroglyph National Monument (all ages)

6001 Unser Boulevard NW (I–40 west to Coors, then Coors to Montano Road; follow the signs). National Park Service: (505) 899–0205, extension 335. Open Space Division of the City of Albuquerque: (505) 873–6620. Information Area on Unser Boulevard and Western Trail Road. www.nps.gov/petr. Open daily from 8:00 A.M. to 5:00 P.M. Admission: $1.00 per vehicle on weekdays, $2.00 on weekends.

This is a great outdoor treat for the kids. Bring a picnic lunch and plenty of water, wear sturdy boots, and spend the day hiking through this park, which traces the development of Native American culture in the Rio Grande Valley from prehistory to the present. Petroglyphs are the strange, mysterious drawings and designs that ancient settlers carved into the rocks and caves where they lived. At the monument, these pictographs of a culture thousands of years old are sculpted into the black, volcanic cliffs of Albuquerque's west side. The park is divided into three main areas: **Boca Negra Canyon, Rinconada Canyon,** and the **Volcanoes;** they are full of wonderful hiking trails, gorgeous canyon vistas, and the petroglyphs themselves. It's well worth taking the children to see. Rangers are available for tours, if you call to arrange in advance. Stop at the ranger center for maps and information.

Shady Lakes (all ages)

11033 Highway 85 NW. Take I–25 east to Tramway Street, go south to Highway 313 west, Shady Lake is ½ mile on the left; (505) 898–2568. Open April through September, 8:00 A.M. to 6:00 P.M. Admission: $4.95 for adults, $2.95 for children under 12 plus 52 cents/inch for what you catch.

Enjoy easy recreational fishing (trout, bluegill, catfish, and bass) nestled in a grove of cottonwood trees. There are beautiful water lily ponds, too.

Sierra Farms (all ages)

In Tijeras, south of town at I–40 and Highway 14 to Highway 337. Go 11 miles to a right turn on Mockingbird Drive, then continue for 100 feet or so; (505) 281–5061. Open Tuesday through Sunday 10:00 A.M. to 5:00 P.M. Free admission; small fee for feeding the animals.

Help feed and corral the baby goats at this charming working goat farm and dairy.

FBI **Building**

415 Silver Avenue NW; (505) 224–2000.

While you're in the center of town, check out this original and fascinating exhibit. You can meet a real FBI agent and get a tour of the facility.

Where to Eat

Flying Star Bakery Cafe. 4501 Juan Tabo; (505) 275–8311, 3416 Central SE; (505) 255–6633, 8001 Menaul; (505) 293–6911, or 4026 Rio Grande; (505) 344–6714. Sandwiches, pastries, quiche, and stir-frys. Open daily 6:00 A.M. to 11:00 P.M. $–$$

La Placita Mexican Restaurant. 208 San Felipe (near Old Town); (505) 247–2204. Good Mexican-American fare. Open daily 11:00 A.M. to 9:00 P.M. $–$$

Little Anita's. 2105 Mountain Road (at Rio Grande); (505) 242–3102. Mexican food in a pleasant setting. Open daily 7:00 A.M. to 9:00 P.M. $–$$

Yanni's Mediterranean Bar. 3109 Central Avenue; (505) 268–9250. Outstanding inexpensive Mediterranean food. Open daily 11:00 A.M. to 10:00 P.M. $–$$$

For More Information

Visitor Bureau. (505) 842–9918 or (800) 733–9918; www.abqcvb.org.

Indian Pueblo Cultural Center. (505) 843–7270.

Where to Stay

Comfort Suites. 900 Louisiana (at Lomas); (505) 255–5566. Adjacent to state fairgrounds, there are 164 large rooms (with separate sitting areas). Complimentary full breakfast, laundry facilities, whirlpool. $$

Courtyard by Marriott. 1920 Yale SE; (505) 843–6600; www.marriott.com. This hotel offers 150 rooms (some suites) near the airport. Indoor pool and hot tub; complimentary in-room coffee and cable television. Restaurant for breakfast only. Sorry, no pets. $$–$$$

Days Inn-East. 13317 Central Avenue NE; (505) 294–3297. Seventy-two rooms fill this hotel near downtown Albuquerque. Indoor pool, whirlpool, sauna, cable television, complimentary continental breakfast. Children under 12 **free**. Small pets OK. $$–$$$

New Mexico Bed and Breakfast Association. (800) 661–6649.

Jémez Mountains Area

I-25 north to Bernalillo exit (Highway 44) to Highway 4 north.

Recently named a scenic byway, Highway 4 is an incredibly beautiful road and makes a nice loop drive from Albuquerque to Bandelier National Monument and Los Alamos (and wherever you would like to go from there!). The Forest Service office, which oversees the monument, is located just below Soda Dam (see below) and has information on the campgrounds and hot springs in the area.

Jémez Pueblo (ages 10 to 12)

Highway 4; 5 miles north of San Isidro (junction of Highway 4 and Highway 44). Walatowa Visitor Center open weekdays 8:00 A.M. to 5:00 P.M.; (505) 834–7235. Walatowa Convenience Store open 6:00 A.M. to 10:00 P.M.

The Jémez Pueblo had the reputation of being the home of some of the fiercest combatants in the Spanish-Indian struggle, but visiting today is a much more pleasant experience than it was for the conquistadors. As you near the pueblo, you may come across the women of the tribe who sometimes set up shop along Highway 4 to sell freshly made fry bread. It's a good idea to stop to sample this delicious confection. On the reservation stop at the Walatowa Visitor Center, where you and your kids can enjoy various interpretive programs, such as bread-baking demonstrations, traditional dance presentations, and pottery making. From April through October, on weekends only, there is an open market where you can see the arts and crafts of the Jémez Indians and sample some of their traditional foods. The pueblo offers fishing and picnicking areas, too. The pueblo is also open to the public during feast days.

Annual **Community Events**

Annual Jémez Pueblo community events are held within the pueblo and include ceremonial dance performances, good food, music, and arts and crafts.

AUGUST 2
St. Persingula's Feast Day and **Old Pecos Bull Ceremony**

DECEMBER 12
Matachine Dances

McCauley **Springs**

A hot spring area (clothes optional!) along the Battleship Rock trail.

Village of Jémez Springs (all ages)
Highway 4, 15 miles from San Isidro or 45 miles from Los Alamos; (505) 829–3540.

This is a good spot to stop for a bite to eat between excursions.

Jémez Springs Bath House (ages 10 to 12)
62 Jémez Springs Plaza, Jémez Springs; (505) 829–3303.

This is a historic bathhouse/spa, built in the 1870s, that can give you a refreshing geothermal experience. There's a gift shop with unique bath accessories.

Jémez State Monument (all ages)
On Highway 4, ¼ mile from Jémez Springs; (505) 829–3530. Open Wednesday through Monday 8:30 A.M. to 5:00 P.M. Admission: $3.00 for those 17 and over.

The monument is on the site of the Giusewewa Ruins, the original site of Jémez Pueblo. There is a seventeenth-century mission church, and the museum is well stocked with Spanish and Native American artifacts.

Soda Dam (all ages) **and Cave** (ages 10 to 12)
On Highway 4; 1 mile north of Jémez Springs. USDA Forest Service: (505) 438–7840. Open year-round. Free.

This is another good vantage spot for viewing the Jémez Mountains. Some historians estimate that there have been humans occupying this calcium carbonate formation since 2500 B.C. You and your kids will notice odd mushroom-shaped rocks surrounding the natural dam. While most people stop to look at the outside of this remarkable travertine rock outcropping, an equally beautiful view of the place is inside the cave. It is a mystical wonderland of layered sediment and fountainlike formations with pools of warm, still water. Be careful; this is a tricky entrance, and the cave is not meant for strollers, backpacks, young children, or open footwear.

If you have little ones, the outside is glorious enough. There are wonderful trails that take you from one marvelous view of the dam to another up through the pink cliffs. The kids can look for 500 million-year-old Precambrian fossils embedded in the cliffs. Bring bathing suits because you can play in the water. No diving, though, because of the hidden rocks below. Again, bring all that you think you will need (and then a bit extra, too).

Battleship Rock (all ages)

Highway 4, 5 miles north of Jémez Springs. USDA Forest Service: (505) 829–3535. Admission: $5.00 for parking.

This hike takes you to a rock outcropping that looks like the prow of a ship jutting out of the mountainside. You can walk on to Jémez Falls (an additional 1½ miles), or drive up to them (see below).

Jémez Falls (all ages)

Highway 4, 7 miles from Jémez Springs, 5 from La Cueva. USDA Forest Service: (505) 829–3535. Admission: $5.00 for parking.

You'll pass the campgrounds first on your right, but continue to the picnic grounds a bit below, where there is parking. To get to the falls, look for the wooden fence at the parking lot and follow it until it gives way to a well-maintained path ¼ mile from the falls. You'll see a less well-kept trail just past the drainage area; this is a 2-mile hike back to McCauley Springs.

Fenton Lake State Park (all ages)

Highway 4 and Highway 126, 19 miles from Jémez Springs; (505) 829–3630. Open year-round. Admission: $5.00 for day use, $10.00 for overnight ($14.00 for hookups).

The area is surrounded by ponderosa pine forests. The park offers Nordic ski facilities, a biathlon trail, and fishing platforms that can accommodate a wheelchair or stroller. *Note:* Highway 126 is rugged and unpaved (at this writing); it is closed during the winter months.

Las Conchas Trail (all ages)

Highway 4, 25 miles from La Cueva. Santa Fe National Forest: (505) 438–7840.

A sweet trail with very little grade along the east fork of the Jémez River. It looks like Switzerland up here. You cross hand-hewn log bridges at various points and can take dips in the river as it keeps you company. The trail is 4 miles long, so you have to determine at what point you want to turn around and head back.

Valle Grande (all ages)

Highway 4, 15 miles from La Cueva.

A 3-by-5-mile-wide volcanic crater now used for grazing.

Where to Eat

Laughing Lizard Cafe and Inn. 17526 Highway 4; (505) 829–3108; www.the laughinglizard.com. Homemade food in adobe cafe; lodging facilities as well. Open Tuesday through Friday 11:00 A.M. to 8:00 P.M. and Sunday 11:00 A.M. to 6:00 P.M. $–$$

Los Ojos Restaurant. Highway 4, Jémez Springs; (505) 829–3547. Local hangout. Open daily 11:00 A.M. to 9:00 P.M. $–$$

Where to Stay

Dancing Bear Bed and Breakfast. 314 San Diego; (505) 829–3336 or (800) 422–3271; www.dancingbearbandb.com. Charming retreat off the beaten path. $–$$

Elk Mountain Lodge. 37485 Highway 126 (Highway 4 ends at Highway 126 farther north); (505) 829–3159 or (800) 815–2859; www.elkmountainlodge.cc. Hideaway and river retreat. $–$$

Jémez Canyon Inn. 17050 Highway 4; (505) 829–3254 or (888) 759–9095. Near fishing, hiking, and hot springs. Courtyard with barbecue facilities. $–$$

For More Information

Jémez Springs Visitor Information. In Jémez Plaza, next to village office; (505) 829–3540. USDA Forest Service: (505) 829–3535.

Rio Rancho

Highway 528 and I–25, north edge of Albuquerque.

A land development project in the 1960s, this is now the fastest growing city in New Mexico due to the presence of some very large employers that have made Rio Rancho their Southwest headquarters.

J & R Vintage Auto Museum (all ages)
3650–A Highway 528; (505) 867–2281; www.jrvintageautos.com. Open Monday through Saturday 10:00 A.M. to 6:00 P.M. (5:00 P.M. in winter). Admission: $4.00 for adults, $3.00 for seniors, $1.50 for children 6–12, under 6 admitted free.

This is 50,000 square feet of antique autos and fire trucks dating from 1903, when levers were used instead of wheels to steer cars.

Blades Multiplex Arena (all ages)
801 Loma Colorado Drive; (505) 892–9222. Hours vary. Admission: $6.00 for adults, $5.00 for children 5 and under. Additional $2.00 to rent skates.

A great place to go for in-line and/or ice skating (two separate rinks)

Intel Museum of the Computer Chip (ages 10 to 12)
1600 Rio Rancho Boulevard; (505) 893–TOUR. Open Monday through Friday 8:00 A.M. to 7:00 P.M. Free.

You knew this was coming. You can take a self-guided tour or arrange for a guide.

For More Information

Visitors Bureau. (888) 746–7262.

Bernalillo

I–25 north to the Bernalillo exit and Highway 44.

The town of Bernalillo is a very modest suburb north of Albuquerque.

Coronado State Monument (all ages)
I–25 north to the Bernalillo exit and Highway 44; (505) 867–5351. Open Wednesday through Monday (except for holidays) from 8:30 A.M. to 5:30 P.M. Admission: $3.00 for adults, children 17 and under free.

On your way to Coronado State Monument, you'll be greeted by a stunning view of the Sandia Mountains. *Sandia* is Spanish for watermelon. If you're lucky enough to drive by the mountain range at sunset, let the kids keep an eye on the changing hues of the mountains as the sun hits them. They'll see the whole range turn a glorious rosy red, like the inside of a perfectly ripe watermelon—thus the name.

The monument in the park commemorates Spanish explorer Francisco Coronado's march into the Rio Grande Valley in 1540. He was one of several adventurers of the time who were convinced that the Indian pueblos were really repositories of gold. The explorers believed that there were seven such areas in this part of the New World, which they called the seven cities of Cibola. Coronado was on the lookout for great riches. Thinking that the now ruined Kuaua Pueblo (the site of this monument) was one of the cities of gold, he advanced on the pueblo. He found nothing but supposedly spent a horrible winter there in 1540, stealing corn from the natives to keep from starving.

In the 1940s archaeologists uncovered layer upon layer of pictographs of Kuaua gods, worship ceremonies, and some of the daily lives of this lost tribe in these ruins. The find proved to be a rare catalogue of clothing, hairstyles, jewelry, foods, and pottery, as well as of the kinds of gods the Kuaua worshiped. Each stratum was carefully removed and preserved. You and your children will be riveted by the variety and detail of these panels, which are preserved in the lovely museum that's located in the middle of the park. There are fifteen panels in all, with intelligent and thorough explanations accompanying them.

If the children get restless, there's a pleasant hiking trail starting at the museum that leads through the ruins of this remarkable pueblo. The settlement had over 1,200 rooms and stood three stories high. The trail leads on to a reconstructed kiva that you and your kids can climb down into and explore at your leisure.

If you and your family want to spend some time in this gorgeous area edging the Rio Grande, the park has more than fifty campsites on a bluff above the river. If you have some time and are returning to Albuquerque, travel the Camino Real, the Royal Road, along the Rio Grande, beneath which lie more than fifteen unexcavated pueblos.

Jackalope (all ages) 🔒

Highway 44; (505) 867–9813. Open Sunday through Thursday 9:00 A.M. to 6:00 P.M.; Friday and Saturday 9:00 A.M. to 7:00 P.M.

This is a terrific *mercado*, or shopping place. It's crammed with colorful, practical goodies from South America: pottery, rugs, trinkets for the kids, even furniture and glassware. The whole family will find something that they can't live without, and you can go home with some inexpensive, but wonderful, gifts.

Our Lady of Sorrows Museum and Gallery (ages 10 to 12) 🖼

301 Camino del Pueblo, (505) 867–5252. Take a left at exit 242 from I–25. After about a mile, take a left at a four-way stop. Redbrick church is 1 block up on the right.

This is a historic adobe church that has been restored as a museum and art gallery. The chapel was originally built in 1716, right on top of what had been a pueblo kiva.

Sandia Pueblo (all ages)

I–25 to Highway 313, 13 miles north of Albuquerque at Bernalillo; (505) 867–3317; www.sandiapueblo.nsn.us.

Sandia Pueblo, settled in 1300, was known originally as Na-fiat, or "sandy, dusty place" in Tiwa. The pueblo is one of the most successful farming communities in the area. Its residents deserted the site in the 1690s, after the reconquest of New Mexico by Spain, and joined the Hopi tribe in what is now Arizona for about sixty years. Presently, the pueblo is really pushing its brand-new casino, which is open night and day, but you and your family may find more interesting things to do in the pueblo's seventy-acre recreation park. There are lakes stocked with trout, bass, and catfish, and at the intersection of I–25 and Tramway, the pueblo has a huge Indian Market center called Bien Muir where you can buy handmade arts and crafts.

Spanish Pueblo and
Territorial Architectural Styles

As you travel through New Mexico, you may come across these dominant architectural styles, and it may be fun to know a bit about them beforehand. Spanish Pueblo is a Spanish adaptation of the Pueblo style. Pueblo Indians usually built their rectangular, flat-roofed buildings using stone covered in adobe, or baked mud. The style is further characterized by a lack of woodwork and rounded edges. Peeled pine tree logs *(vigas)* were used for beams and were placed about 2 feet apart over the tops of the walls. In between went the *latillas*, or striplings, either in a parallel or herringbone pattern. Dried brush was layered on next, then dirt was (gently) tamped down on top of it all and sloped to direct the rain or melted snow into the spouts jutting out from the connection of the wall and roofs *(canales)*. The Spaniards copied the style somewhat, using the basic model but using adobe bricks (composed of clay and dirt and reenforced with hay) instead of stone, an indoor fireplace fitted into a corner *(kiva)*, and a stone foundation rather than an earthen floor. They also almost always incorporated a portal, or covered porch, into the design. Later, like a mini plaza, these buildings grew and were positioned so that their portals faced each other surrounding a patio, or inner courtyard. It was a good defensive style not only against the probable Indian raids, but also the harsh winters.

It is not simply coincidence that the Santa Fe Trail was established in the same year (1821) that Spain withdrew (after being kicked out) from Mexico. The United States began immediately to pursue trade with Mexico once Spain was no longer an influence. There were now more people, more ideas, and more materials coming through the area and staying. Architecture began to reflect this infusion of European taste and was defined as "Territorial" after the United States annexed New Mexico as a territory in the mid-1840s. Hard bricks from the east, first used for repairs, then for decoration, slowly took over as the adobe (which eventually disintegrates) was replaced. Manufactured windows replaced the handmade ones, and the vigas and the supports of the portal were no longer simply logs, but ornately carved beams and columns. Stucco and lime were later added to protect the bricks.

When did the Spanish first arrive in New Mexico and why?

In 1527 a Spanish galleon, part of an expedition to colonize what is now northern Florida, sank off the coastal waters of Texas, near present-day Brownsville. Four men survived and trekked west to Mexico. When they returned, their leader, Cabeza de Baca, wrote a report of their travels. In it, there are stories the travelers heard from the local natives about seven cities of gold. The government of New Spain (Mexico at the time) sent a priest, Fra Marcos de Niza, to scout out the area, taking one of the survivors, Esteban, with him as a guide. The priest returned and said that he had seen one of the cities, that it was in fact the least of the seven, and that it would take an army to subdue the area. An army was sent in 1540, under the direction of Francisco Vasquez de Coronado, who would have been happy to find just one of the fabled cities. Coronado traveled the area as far as present-day Kansas until 1542, when he realized that he had failed to find any of them and returned home. Despite the failure of his mission, Coronado is credited with being the first Anglo to explore the area and gather information on the peoples and resources there. During the next fifty-six years, attempts by self-motivated Spaniards to colonize the area failed. The region was not secured for Spain until 1598, under Don Juan de Oñate. *Note:* The treasured lands are also known as the seven cities of Cibola (Cibola is thought to be one of the pueblo names that the survivors of the shipwreck heard and translated as "Land of the Buffalo").

Santa Ana Pueblo (all ages)
Highway 44, 12 miles northwest of Bernalillo; (505) 867–3301.

This pueblo is divided into two areas. One is the old Santa Ana Pueblo, which is rarely open to the public, but you and your children can visit the village on New Year's Day, Easter, and Christmas Day. On these holy days, the pueblo does not allow any photographs, sketching, or recording of the proceedings. The other part of the pueblo is the new village, where the pueblo's residents farm and where you will find a food and craft center, called the Ta'ma'ya Cooperative Association, a gorgeous golf course, and the Jémez Canyon Road Dam and Recreation Area.

San Felipe Pueblo (ages 10 to 12)
I–25, about 10 miles north of Bernalillo; (505) 867–3381.

During the May 1 annual feast day celebration dances, the residents set up booths for foods and crafts. Their dances are some of the most beautiful in New Mexico, and your children will be awed and delighted by them. The ancestral home is on the Pajarito Plateau (near Los Alamos), and the village was established in the early eighteenth century.

The pueblo's **Casino Hollywood** and its new **Hollywood Hills Speedway** are two visible additions to the pueblo's business enterprises. The tribe calls the Speedway "New Mexico's Premier Outdoor Entertainment Venue." The facility offers auto and motorcycle racing, concerts, monster truck shows, rodeos, and more. (505) 867–6700.

Santo Domingo Pueblo (ages 10 to 12)
I–25 north to Santo Domingo exit (Highway 22); (505) 465–2214.

Santo Domingo Pueblo is close to Albuquerque and extends to the Cerrillos turquoise mines. It was here that Don Juan de Oñate was granted permission in 1598 to occupy the area. This was also used as the central meeting place for the mission friars who were dispatched over northern New Mexico.

On the feast day of Saint Dominic, August 4, the Santo Domingo Indians perform a stunning Corn Dance that will deeply impress your family. It is an internationally recognized celebration, and the crowds are large. Your kids can visit the various arts and crafts booths, sample delicious native foods, and enjoy the carnival set up for the day. *Caution:* This is a restrained pueblo. Please review the etiquette for attendees referenced in the introduction to this book.

You can also take your kids to the museum and arts and crafts center located on the pueblo, but if you visit on Labor Day weekend, you and your kids will get to enjoy the Santo Domingo Arts and Crafts Market. People come from everywhere in the state to participate in this celebration full of food, dances, and wonderful artifacts.

Belen and Vicinity

I–25 at exit 190.

The town of Belen (Spanish for Bethlehem) is another place that began as a land grant and grew when it was used as a stop on the railroad line. The area around Belen is agricultural, quiet, and quite lovely, but there's not that much to do except get off I–25 if you need to get some gas or grab something to eat.

Harvey House Museum (ages 10 to 12)
104 North First Street; (505) 861–0581. Open Tuesday through Sunday 12:30 P.M. to 3:30 P.M. Admission: by donation.

The museum serves as a repository for railroad history, and your kids will find it interesting. It also sings the praises of the Harvey House restaurants (it was formerly the Belen

Harvey House). These hotels offered good food and clean rooms to those travelers of long ago and became famous throughout the West for their quality. The renowned Harvey Girls, the waitresses in these celebrated restaurants, are also prominent in this museum, with a perfect replica of a boardinghouse room that housed the girls. Your kids will be impressed that these young women served as pioneers in the emancipation of women.

Chavez Farm Museum (all ages)
Highway 309; (505) 864–8354. Open Monday through Saturday 9:00 A.M. to 5:00 P.M., Sunday 1:00 to 5:00 P.M. Admission: $6.00 for adults, children 5 and under free.
This is the place to go if you and your kids want a glance at a really funky setup that's a cross between Victorian farm life and a modern treasure trove. Full of antiques, wonderful old cars, farm tools and machines, and a collection of Barbie dolls, the farm is another of those one-of-a-kind repositories of stuff your kids won't believe existed. They'll love the cars especially. The owners are on the premises all the time, because this museum is part of their home, so the kids can ask all the questions they want. It's a lot of fun here.

For More Information

Chamber of Commerce and Visitors' Bureau.
(505) 864–8091; www.belennm.com.

Mountainair

From Albuquerque, take I–25 south to U.S. Highway 60 (becomes Main Street) east.

Although it's quite rural, it's really a day trip from Albuquerque. The road winds through the foothills of the Manzano Mountains, through lovely stands of cottonwood trees and junipers, and by the occasional general store. The town was founded in 1903 and built on the Belen cutoff, a shortcut of the Atchison, Topeka & Santa Fe Railroad. Homesteaders arrived and began farming. The area became known as the Pinto Bean Capital of the World, until severe drought caused farmland to be redefined as ranchland. The livestock industry still sustains the community. The main attractions are the Salinas National Monument and the Manzano State Park.

Salinas National Monument (all ages)
Highway 55 in the Manzano Mountains; (505) 847–2585. Open daily 9:00 A.M. to 5:00 P.M.
This is a favorite outing for city families, so bring a picnic lunch. Before you go out, though, stop at the visitor center in the Shaffer Hotel (102 Main Street, Mountainair). There you will get all the directions and information that will make a visit to the monument the best that it can be.

The area was inhabited for centuries by both Indian and Spanish settlers. Although priests built missions along the foothills of the mountains and Native Americans settled pueblos there, the hardships of living through drought and famine and Apache raids caused both groups of settlers to abandon the area. Over the centuries the whole site fell into disrepair and became the ruins that you and your family will visit.

The tract was once a vast salt lake that eventually dried out and left behind huge salt flats, called the "salt missions." If your children have never seen the moonscape of a salt flat gleaming white in the hot sun, they will be quite amazed with these.

The monument comprises three separate ruins:

- **Quarai.** 1 mile west of Highway 55 and 8 miles north of Mountainair (look for turn at the village of Punto de Agua). The most beautiful and most visited area, it is nestled into the eastern foothills of the Manzano Mountains. The church (built mostly by Indian women and children from 1626 to 1628), la Purisima Concepcion de Cuarar, has 40-foot red sandstone walls that are 5 feet thick in places. It is the most completely preserved example of a seventeenth-century Spanish Franciscan mission.

- **Gran Quivira.** Highway 55, 25 miles south of Mountainair. The site had a complex of buildings, including two churches, that contained nearly 3,000 rooms. The pueblo was surrounded by well-engineered irrigation systems and terraces for growing corn, squash, even cotton. Salt was the main trading commodity.

- **Abó.** Highway 513, 9 miles west of Mountainair, ½ mile north of US 60. Located along a spring at a narrow mountain pass, the site features San Gregorio Church, one of the most architecturally sophisticated buildings of its time (it was completed in 1651). Picnic facilities are available.

Manzano Mountains State Park (all ages)

Highway 337, 13 miles west of Mountainair, then 3 miles southwest on Forest Service Road 253. Park Manager's Office: (505) 847–2820. Admission: $5.00 for day use, $10.00 for overnight ($4.00 for hookups).

The Tajique Torreon Loop is a rugged, challenging outdoor adventure (and one of the lesser-known charms of this area). The road takes you through the Manzano Mountains wilderness area. There are lots of trails and great views of the countryside. It is especially lovely during autumn.

Fourth of July Campground

(505) 847–2990 (USDA Forest Service, Mountainair Ranger District). From Tijeras, take Route 337 south 30 miles until it comes to a "T"; take a right on Highway 55 and go another 8 miles.

The campground offers picnic areas if you want a few hours in the outdoors.

Where to Eat

Ancient Cities Cafe. Highway 60; (505) 847–2368. Mexican food, hamburgers, and sandwiches. Open daily 6:00 A.M. to 9:00 P.M., Sunday 8:00 A.M. to 9:00 P.M. $

Where to Stay

Shaffer Hotel. 103 Main Street; (505) 847–2888; www.shafferhotel.com. National historic site under new ownership, restored to its original charm. Twenty-two rooms, elegant setting, and exquisite food define the Shaffer. Beautiful art throughout. Check out the Rancho Bonito, 2 miles south of the hotel where "Pop" Shaffer created a little work of art (he also decorated those concrete fence posts at the hotel). $$

For More Information

Chamber of Commerce. (505) 847–2795; www.mountainairchamber.com.

North Central
New Mexico

The north central portion of New Mexico is the heart of the state and a delightful example of its famous tricultural Spanish, Native American, and Anglo life. The great Native American pueblos of Taos, Santa Clara, and San Ildefonso are within driving distance of New Mexico's beautiful state capital, Santa Fe. On top of that, your family can enjoy other area delights: inexpensive skiing, fascinating museums, a working eighteenth-century colonial farm, lakes, forests, mountains, movie sets, and a walk along the famous Santa Fe Trail.

For much of the twentieth century, Santa Fe and its surroundings were home to many internationally acclaimed people, such as artist Georgia O'Keeffe, author D.H. Lawrence, and physicist Enrico Fermi. Many famous contemporary writers, artists, and actors make their homes here as well.

In Taos, your children can visit Kit Carson's home, see what an eighteenth-century walled farmhouse looks like, and ski some wonderful mountain trails.

There's also the famous town of Los Alamos, where the whole family can learn about the making of the atomic bomb at the Bradbury Science Museum.

This is an area rich in the history and art of the Southwest, crammed full of some of the best sites and sights that New Mexico has to offer.

NORTH CENTRAL

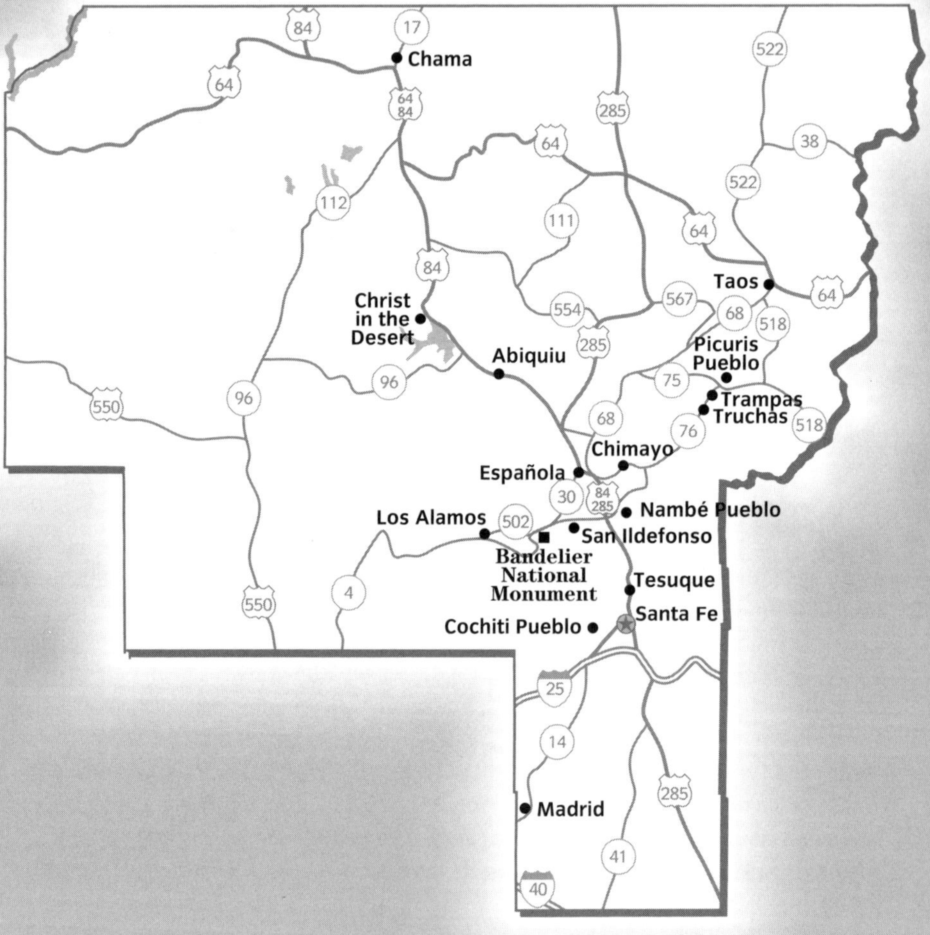

84
17
● **Chama**
64
522
64
84
285
64
38
112
522
111
64
84
554
567
Taos ●
285
68
518
64
Christ in the Desert ●
Abiquiu ●
75
Picuris Pueblo
96
96
68
76
● **Trampas**
Truchas
518
550
Chimayo
Española ●
84
285
30
Los Alamos ●
502
● **Nambé Pueblo**
■ **San Ildefonso**
Bandelier National Monument
4
Tesuque
550
Cochiti Pueblo ●
★ **Santa Fe**
25
14
285
● **Madrid**
41
40

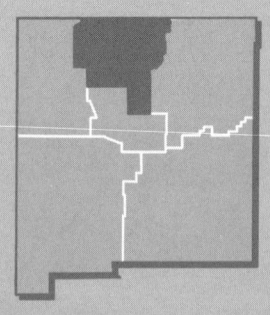

Taos Area

The area around Taos packs a lot of punch because of its very old history. (It also has more art studios and galleries per capita than anywhere else in the United States.) It is really three centers in one. First, there is the Taos Pueblo, then the village of Taos, and finally the small farming area known as Ranchos de Taos, which was founded before the Europeans arrived.

Taos Pueblo (all ages)

U.S. Highway 64, 3 miles north of Taos; (505) 758–1028. Open daily 8:00 A.M. to 4:30 P.M. Admission: $10.00 for adults, $5.00 for students; guided tours every ½ hour from 9:00 A.M. to 4:00 P.M. (payment by gratuity).

Taos Pueblo is considered the oldest continually inhabited Native American site in the country. In 1993 it was named a World Heritage Site by the United Nations. It has been in existence, in one form or another, for at least 1,000 years. The sprawling adobe structures have figured in the paintings, drawings, and photographs of literally hundreds of artists. A visit here is an absolute must for the kids. They'll get to see, firsthand, an ancient way of life. **Note:** While the pueblo appears open and relaxed, note that you and your children are entering a special world. Don't go into any home or structure that is closed or private, find out under what conditions you may take pictures, and never wade in the stream that flows through the pueblo. This is the Rio Pueblo de Taos and is both a sacred river used in ceremonies and the tribe's only source of drinking water.

Taos Pueblo **Ceremonial Dances**

Try to plan your trip to include one of these memorable dances. They are all performed outdoors, and sometimes there are long waits between the sets while the performers rest or pray. Take water and wear clothing appropriate for the season. You can buy snacks on the pueblo. Call the Taos Pueblo for exact times, locations, and fees.

- **New Year's Day Celebration.** A mass, dances, and a procession. *New Year's Day*

- **Santa Cruz Feast Day.** A blessing of the fields, a corn dance, games, and good food. *Late May or early June*

- **Taos Pueblo Feast Day.** Vespers at San Jerome Chapel and a Sundown Dance, followed by a feast dedicated to San Geronimo and a mass the next morning, dancing, games, and pole-climbing by the Pueblo clown-figures, the Koshares. *Late September*

D. H. Lawrence **Memorial**

San Cristobal, 12 miles north of Taos on Highway 522. No restroom or telephone available—go during the day.

This is a lovely place to take the family. The British writer's ashes are buried in this charming adobe building that is surrounded by huge spruce trees and a vast ranch. The land is owned by the University of New Mexico, and while the memorial is open to the public, the rest of the area is not.

Presently the huge buildings are showing their age. While you and your family can certainly imagine its once magnificent stature, the pueblo looks a bit worn. Nonetheless, the children will be able to go into some of the small, attached houses and talk with the Tewa-Taos Indians, who will discuss a way of life that they still live.

The oldest buildings have walls that connect with each other but no doorways, because hundreds of years ago the entrances were on the roof and residents got in and out of their homes by ladders. There are still about 200 Taos Native Americans who live according to tribal custom without running water or electricity in these ancient structures (the rest live in modern housing dotted throughout the pueblo).

As you take your kids around, keep an eye out for the hornos, outdoor ovens for baking traditional breads. In the houses that are open to the public, be sure to look up at the ceilings. Have your kids notice the vigas (large, tree-size beams) and latillas (the small branches set between the vigas).

Rio Grande Gorge Bridge (all ages)
US 64 between Taos Pueblo and the village of Taos.

Your children will have a hair-raising experience walking across the second-highest expansion bridge in the United States. It is heart-stopping to peer down 650 feet into the Rio Grande Gorge, with the Rio Grande itself a mere ribbon of water. If you and your kids are lucky (or unlucky!), you may catch a daredevil pilot flying under the bridge. No matter; it's a glorious treat to walk across and test your mettle. You may see people climbing down into the gorge. While you might like to try this, be warned—this is not a casual hike.

Whitewater **Rafting**

The Rio Grande Gorge offers some exciting possibilities. Several rafting groups will take you down this famous river. Call **Far Flung Adventures** (505–758–2628) or **Los Rios River Runners** (505–776–8854) to arrange a trip.

Kids under 13 probably won't enjoy it, and this is not something to do if you have little outdoor experience. If you want to try it, wear appropriate clothing and footwear, bring water and food, and be prepared for an arduous climb both down and up.

Village of Taos and Vicinity
US 64 at Highway 68, about 1½ hours from Santa Fe.

The Spanish came in 1598 with the famous conquistador Juan de Oñate. They settled the region but were constantly battling with the Taos Pueblo Indians. Finally, the natives rose up against the Spaniards in the Pueblo Revolt of 1680. Twelve years later, Don Diego de Vargas returned and resettled the whole of northern New Mexico. Later in Taos's history, Anglo settlers entered the picture, especially in the person of the famous Kit Carson. Take time to walk Taos Plaza, and visit the sites of some of the more famous residents. The Museum Association oversees seven of the museums in town and offers special admission rates to them based on three (the Blumenshein, the Hacienda Martinez, and the Kit Carson Home and Museum) or all seven (add the Harwood, the Van Vechten–Lineberry [two art museums], the Governor Bent House, and the Nicolai Fechin Institute). These passes can be purchased at any of the museums and are good for a year.

Taos Plaza (all ages)

Take one of the self-guided tours through what was once the heart of the early village of Taos. Now it is armed with restaurants and gift shops, but the kids can certainly get an idea of what an old Hispanic town plaza looked like while they walk under the adobe porticos of the buildings. Most of the towns in the West began with a plaza surrounded by buildings for protection, in similar formation to the Conestoga wagons when they were under attack. The saloon was the central meeting place and sometimes began as a parked Conestoga wagon.

El Paso **Llama Expeditions**

(800) 4–llamas; www.elpaseollama.com. Llama trekking for the whole family. All gear provided.

Hacienda Martinez (ages 10 to 12)

2 miles west of Taos Plaza on Ranchitos Road; (505) 758–1000. Open daily from 9:00 A.M. to 5:00 P.M. Admission: $5.00 for adults, $3.00 for children under 16.

This is a good example of a fortified farm and is one of the few remaining original Spanish colonials still open to the public. The twenty rooms were built around two courtyards, then surrounded by a thick wall to keep the family and workers safe from Indian attack. The hacienda is unadorned but worth investigating. Included in the restored areas are storage spaces, a kitchen, and a bedroom/living room. The gift shop has a lot of children's books that explain some of the traditions and stories from this period.

Kit Carson Home and Museum (ages 10 to 12)

113 Kit Carson Road (US 64 east), across from Highway 68 coming from Taos Plaza; (505) 758–4741. Open daily from 9:00 A.M. to 5:00 P.M. Admission: $5.00 for adults, $3.00 for children under 16.

Here you and the children will be able to see the rooms that Kit and his family lived in. Each is decorated with the furniture and in the style of the period. There are also displays of guns, artifacts, and equipment of the Old West that your kids will enjoy.

Kit Carson Park and Cemetery (all ages)

2 blocks north of Kit Carson Home and Museum on Highway 68.

This is where the remains of Kit Carson and his family are buried, along with those of Mabel Dodge Lujan (a former East Coast socialite and Taos resident who was instrumental in the beginnings of the Taos artistic community) and the soldiers who fought in the 1847 rebellion against the U.S. annexation of New Mexico, among others. The park is a pleasant place to rest for a bit. There are slides and swings to entertain the children while you take a break.

Day Trip: **Enchanted Circle**

This 84-mile round-trip is a remarkable experience. The Chamber of Commerce has maps and details of the trip, which starts in Taos, then takes you east through the Taos canyon, the 9,000-foot Palo Flechado ("Arrow") Pass, and the towns of Angel Fire, Eagles Nest, Questa, San Cristobal, and Arroyo Hondo. Bring plenty of food and water, and enjoy. You'll discover some lovely small towns and breathtaking scenery.

Pueblo Balloon **Company**

(505) 751–9877; www.puebloballoon.com. Balloon rides over the Rio Grande Gorge.

Governor Bent House and Museum (ages 10 to 12)

117 Bent Street, 1 block north of Taos Plaza off Highway 68; (505) 758–2376. Open daily from 10:00 A.M. to 5:00 P.M. Admission: $2.00 for adults, $1.00 for children 8–15.

In the town's more elegant section, with charming boutiques, pleasant eateries, art galleries, and clothing shops, is the Governor Bent House and Museum. This is not a fancy place. It is a bit dusty and cluttered, but it is the home of New Mexico's first American governor. He lived here with his wife and family, hoping to serve as a bridge connecting the three cultures of Indian, Spanish, and Anglo settlers. Unfortunately, the Indians saw him as an enemy and killed him. The kids will enjoy talking with the knowledgeable guide (who also mans the tiny gift shop) and find it moving to see the site where Bent's wife tried to dig through the wall to help the family escape from the siege that killed her husband.

Taos Art Museum and Fechin House (ages 10 to 12)

227 Paseo del Pueblo Norte, off Highway 68, just after Kit Carson Park; (505) 758–2690. Open Tuesday through Sunday 10:00 A.M. to 5:00 P.M. Admission: $6.00.

Here the Russian artist Nicolai Fechin lived with his wife and daughter, Eya. Fechin made almost all of the furniture here in a very Russian style, and you and your children will delight in the charm of this lovely house.

Blumenshein Home (all ages)

222 Ledoux Street, 2 blocks west of Taos Plaza; (505) 758–0505. Open daily from 9:00 A.M. to 5:00 P.M. Admission: $5.00 for adults, $3.00 for children under 16.

This is another artist's home to visit. It is a wonderful experience for all the family—even younger children will enjoy it. The house is almost exactly as it was when the Blumenshein family lived here. They were all artists. Paintings and drawings of parents Ernest and Mary and their daughter, Helen, are hung throughout the rooms. The kitchen is a great place for the kids to see—no microwave, no double-door refrigerator, no built-in stove—just a kitchen precisely as it was in the 1920s, complete with spice boxes and flour bags.

Skiing

Skiing is a big draw in the area. There are four mountains within an hour of Taos. The season lasts from approximately Thanksgiving to Easter, depending on the weather conditions; all lifts are in operation daily from 9:00 A.M. to 4:00 P.M. Lodging is available on all of the mountains. I strongly suggest tapping into the resorts' Web sites for current special rates and/or activities (they are happy to speak to you, too). Also, check out the chairlift rides during the summer; they are a beautiful and effortless way to see some magnificent views.

- **Angel Fire.** From Taos: Take US 64 east for 24 miles; take a right at Route 434, then follow signs to Angel Fire; (800) 633–7463 or (505) 377–6410; www.skiangelfire.com. Angel Fire has a Nordic center, a snowboarding park (snowboarding on the mountain is permitted, but jumping is not), sleigh rides, snowblading, and snowmobiles. Child care is available for children ages 6 weeks to 10 years (bring immunization records) by the hour or half or full day. Call (505) 377–6410 for reservations. There is a ski/snowboarding school for all ages (no one in diapers, though). People over 65 ski for free. After hours (5:30 to 7:30 P.M.) the mountain is fully lit, and everyone (no age limit) can ride inner tubes down the slopes.

- **Red River.** Route 522 north to Questa. At the signal light in Questa (there's only one), take a right and go east about 11 miles to Red River on Highway 38; (800) 331–SNOW (7669) (lodging and rental packages), (505) 754–2223 (skiing conditions), (505) 754–2220 (snow report); redriverskiarea.com. Child care is available for kids 6 months to 4 years, for half or full days. There is also a Youth Ski Club for kids from 4 years that offers full-day packages (lunch included) of lessons and practice.

- **Taos Ski Valley.** Take US 64 north for 13 miles. At intersection with Route 150 east, turn right and continue another 11 miles. Road dead-ends in parking lot; (800) 776–1111 or (800) 347–7414 (reservations and information), (505) 776–1111 (snow conditions); www.skitaos.org; e-mail: tsv@skitaos.org. Taos Ski Valley considers itself unique in that it offers straight alpine skiing. There are links, however, to other areas and businesses nearby for those who want to snowboard, snowmobile, or cross-country ski. The mountain is steeper than most. There is inner tubing at night (6:00 to 8:00 P.M., $5.00 per person). For child care, there is Babycare for infants, Kindercare for toddlers not yet potty-trained. Two Junior Elite groups are available for 4- and 5-year-olds and first graders through 12 years. The older groups get into as much or as little ski schooling as you would like.

El Rincón Trading Post and Museum (ages 10 to 12)

Kit Carson Road; (505) 758–9188. Open daily from 10:00 A.M. to 5:00 P.M. Admission: Free.

This is an amazingly cluttered but fascinating emporium that was Taos's original trading post. It's piled high with the jewelry, beads, drums, feathers, and pots you'd expect to find in a place like this. In the back, there's a room filled with artifacts of Taos's long history. Bring the kids here to give them a peek at an enterprise that makes few concessions to the tourist industry.

The Fire House Collection (all ages)

Bent Street, 2 blocks north at the corner of Armory Street and Placitas Road; (505) 758–3386. Open weekdays only from 8:00 A.M. to 5:00 P.M. Admission: Free.

The building actually houses the Taos Volunteer Fire Department. If you have kids who moan and groan at the thought of an art gallery, this may be a positive introduction to the artistic world. Not only does it have five fully equipped fire engines (which the kids can take a look at), but it also has more than a hundred paintings by local artists. There's also an antique engine.

San Francisco de Asis Church (ages 10 to 12)

In Ranchos de Taos; (505) 758–2754. Open daily (except Sunday) from 9:00 A.M. to 4:00 P.M. Admission: Free.

Visit this charming, earthy church, which is quickly recognizable if you are a Georgia O'Keeffe fan (she made it famous in some of her paintings). If you search out one of these images in an art book and show it to your kids before you set off, they'll be truly impressed seeing the work of art and then the real thing. Be sure to visit the rectory hall across from the church. The famous painting there by Henri Ault called *Shadow of the Cross* will touch even the most exhausted child. In daylight, the picture looks ordinary, but in the dark it begins to glow, outlining the figure of Jesus just as, over his left shoulder, the clouds begin to form a shadow in the shape of a cross. It's a showstopper.

Wheeler **Peak**

West of Eagle Nest, this mountain, at 13,161 feet, is the highest point in New Mexico.

Carson National Forest (all ages)

Ranger Station: (505) 758–6200; www.fs.fed.us/r3/carson.

Taos has an active outdoor life pretty much dominated by the Carson National Forest. This huge wilderness has some wonderful fishing lakes, many interesting hiking trails, and campsites as well. Because it's a fairly rugged forest, RVs are not suited to its roads, and it is so big that it is strongly advised that you first visit the park's Web site or call the ranger station.

Tres Piedras State Wildlife Area (all ages)

US 64 west to U.S. Highway 285 south, about 30 miles from Taos; (505) 758–8678.

For wildlife viewing, "Three Rocks" offers 3,300 acres. In the fall and early winter, your kids can spot elk and antelope from the road (there is a viewing area on US 285).

Where to Eat

Apple Tree Restaurant. 123 Bent Street; (505) 758–1900. Eclectic southwestern menu in a lovely adobe building. Children's menu. All baked goods prepared on the premises. Open 11:30 A.M. to 3:00 P.M. and 5:00 P.M. to 9:00 P.M. $–$$$

Michael's Kitchen. 305 Paseo del Pueblo Norte; (505) 758–4178. Casual, hearty food. Breakfast served all day. Sandwiches, chicken, burgers served with or without a bit of Southwestern flavor. Open 7:00 A.M. to 8:30 P.M. $–$$

Stakeout Grill and Bar. Stakeout Drive (8 miles south of Taos off Highway 68; (505) 758–2042. Pick a nice day to sit outside and enjoy the spectacular views of the Sangre de Cristo Mountains while live music plays. Excel-

lent continental menu (one for children, too). Reservations recommended. Open daily 5:00 P.M. to closing. $$–$$$

Where to Stay

Fechin Inn. 227 Paseo Pueblo Norte (US 64); (505) 751–1000 or (800) 811–2933; www.fechininn.com. Adjacent to Kit Carson Park, this elegant eighty-four room inn is inspired by the art and located on the grounds of Russian-born artist and builder Nicolai Fechin. Laundry, child care, hot tub, fitness facilities, and massage services available. Restaurant and lounge nearby. Small pets welcome. $$–$$$

Kachina Lodge Best Western. 413 Paseo Pueblo Norte (US 64); (505) 758–2275 or (800) 522–4462; www.kachinalodge.com. Within walking distance of the plaza, it includes 118 spacious southwestern-style guest rooms, some with kitchenettes. Restaurant, lounge, outdoor pool, hot tub on site. Nightly Native American dances from May through October. No pets. $$$

Ramada Inn. 615 Paseo Pueblo Sur (Highway 68); (505) 758–2900 or (800) 2–RAMADA. There are 124 modern rooms with balconies (some with fireplaces), a restaurant and bar on premises (open for breakfast, lunch, and dinner), game room, and whirlpool. Pets welcome. Children under 18 **free.**

Taos Bed and Breakfast Association. (800) 939–2215.

RESERVATION COMPANIES

Taos Central Reservations. (800) 821–2437.

Taos Valley Resort Association. (800) 776–1111.

For More Information

Taos Chamber of Commerce and Visitors Bureau. (505) 758–3873 or (800) 732–8267; www.taoschamber.com; www .taos.org.

Annual Community Events

MAY
Taos Spring Arts Festival. Various locations; (505) 758–3873. Three weeks of performing and visual art.

LATE SEPTEMBER
Old Taos Trade Fair. Hacienda Martinez; (505) 758–0505. Spanish colonial lifestyle comes to life.

DECEMBER
Yuletide in Taos. Throughout Taos; (800) 732–8267 or (505) 758–3873. Includes *farolito* tours (walking tours through streets lit only by these small lanterns), ski valley celebrations, and general gaiety.

Picuris Pueblo **Ceremonial Dances**

There are many feast days celebrated at the pueblo, but the most important is the Feast of San Lorenzo (August 10). Check out the dances and the pole-climbing.

Picuris Pueblo

Highway 68 to Highway 75 east, in Penasco, 25 miles south of Taos; (505) 587–2519.

This smallest of New Mexico's nineteen pueblos is charming. The name in Tiwa (a variation of Tewa) means "Those Who Paint." The Native Americans who live here are part of the same Tewa tribe as the Taos Pueblo Indians. There are **free,** self-guided tours of the 700-year-old kivas and the small museum.

San Lorenzo Church (ages 10 to 12)

Before you and your family leave the Picuris Pueblo, be sure to visit the church. Originally completed in 1776, it was recently restored, a sixteen-year project. The final touch will be the restoration of the colorful altar screen. Various groups, clubs, and church organizations have pledged time to help with the rebuilding. You and your family are welcome to join in.

Trampas

Highway 76, 20 miles northeast of Española.

This is an area of truly gorgeous natural beauty. Trampas is one of those very small, very old, back-road towns that give you and your kids a taste of what old New Mexico was like. There are families who have lived in the village for hundreds of years. There are no places to eat or shop, though.

FYI

The state animal is the black bear, and the state bird is the roadrunner.

San Jose Church (ages 10 to 12)

The centerpiece of Trampas is this lovely adobe church, which has figured into innumerable paintings that describe northern New Mexico.

For More Information

State of New Mexico Tourist Office.
(800) 733–6396; www.newmexico.org.

Truchas

Highway 76, 17 miles northeast of Española.

This is a delightful little village that was originally set up in the shape of a square to ward off Indian attacks from the north. The area has caught the fancy of many artists, sculptors, and craftspeople. As you drive through the hamlet, you may want to stop in some of the shops, which are also the artists' homes. Some of their work is modern and full of fun that the children will enjoy while you browse through the more serious artifacts. Truchas, meaning "trouts," is also famous for the setting of some of the scenes in Robert Redford's movie *The Milagro Beanfield War.* If you ask the local residents, they'll gladly point out the area where the filming took place.

Santa Cruz Lake Recreation Area (all ages)
Highway 76, 6 miles east to Highway 503, then south for another 4 miles.
Contact Bureau of Land Management: (505) 758–8851. Open year-round.
Admission: $5.00 for day, $9.00 for overnight.

This is a great place for fishing and camping. There are two campgrounds: The main one is on the lakefront and is considered developed; the other is at the Santa Cruz lookout. There are nature trails around the lake, which is stocked with trout.

For More Information

State of New Mexico Tourist Office.
(800) 733–6396; www.newmexico.org.

Chimayó

Highway 76, 10 miles east of Española.

This village, popular with residents of northern New Mexico, is known for its weaving traditions.

Plaza del Cerro (all ages)
This illustrates the typical Spanish colonial plaza better than any other in New Mexico.

Santuario de Chimayó (all ages)
Highway 520; (505) 351–4889. Open daily from 9:00 A.M. to 5:00 P.M.

Not only is this delightful church, built between 1816 and 1819, a must for photographers and artists, it is a sacred shrine, considered the Lourdes of the Southwest. Here, in the back room, is a hole in the ground that has what many believe to be miraculous dirt. On Good Friday, pilgrims walk from all over the state to this shrine to pray, ask for cures, and take home some of the holy soil. Your children will get a glimpse of little tin pieces tacked on the walls and beams of the church. These are *milagros* ("miracles"), tin shapes of hands, feet, eyes, legs, and various other parts of the body. When believers feel they have been cured of some ailment with this sacred soil, they buy one of these shapes and put it on the wall in thanksgiving for the healing.

Ortega's (ages 10 to 12)
Highway 76; (505) 351–2288 or (800) 743–5921; www.ortegasdechimayo.com. Open Monday through Saturday 9:00 A.M. to 5:00 P.M., Sunday 11:00 A.M. to 5:00 P.M. In winter, closed on Sunday.

If you want to buy gifts such as hand-loomed placemats or clothing, visit this shop. It belongs to the famous Ortega family, who have been weaving cloth for eight generations. Prices are high, but almost all of the fabric is hand-loomed. There's a small room off to the side of the main store where you and the kids can see workers making the cloth. The kids can ask all the questions they want of the weavers and gain some interesting knowledge.

Where to Eat

Leona's Restaurante. Next door to the Santuario de Chimayó; (505) 351–4569; www.leonasrestaurant.com. Excellent tamales and tortillas. Open Thursday through Sunday 11:00 A.M. to 5:00 P.M. $

Rancho de Chimayó. Santa Fe County Road 98; (505) 351–4444. Terrace dining in an old hacienda. Children's menu. Mexican-American cuisine. Open daily 11:30 A.M. to 9:00 P.M. $–$$

Where to Stay

Chimayó Campground. Highway 76, 8 miles outside Española; (505) 351–4566. Hookups and laundry facilities. This may be a good place to stop for the night before heading off to other adventures. $–$$

For More Information

State of New Mexico Tourist Office. (800) 733–6396; www.newmexico.org.

Española

US 285/84 to Highway 68, 25 miles north of Santa Fe.

This is more a highway town offering a lot of chain food restaurants and gas stations than any kind of tourist attraction! Now known as the Capital of Low Riders, it was originally the capital of New Mexico (1598) and is still considered a central point from which you can travel farther south to Santa Fe and Los Alamos, head east to visit some famous pueblos, or head northwest to the famous Cumbres & Toltec Scenic Railroad in Chama.

Santa Clara Pueblo and Puyé Cliff Dwellings (all ages)
Highway 30, 2 miles southwest of Española; (505) 753–7326.

Santa Clara Pueblo is famous for its black carved pottery. The kids will enjoy walking through the pueblo, but even more interesting for them would be a guided tour, which you can schedule through the pueblo's business office. A traditional Native meal at a Santa Clara home can also be arranged after the tour if you make your reservations a week in advance. Another interesting thing to do with your kids is pack a picnic lunch and

Nambéware

In 1951 this eight-metal alloy, which contains no silver, lead, or pewter, was created somewhat by accident at the labs in Los Alamos. Amateur scientist Jane Cable figured out that this stuff was not only beautiful but also practical as cookware since it held its heat for long periods and could also be used in the freezer. Nambéware has become the obligatory giftware for New Mexican weddings and other commemorative events. Check out the Nambé shops in Santa Fe at 104 West San Francisco Street (505–988–3574) and 924 Paseo de Peralta (505–988–5528).

go to the pueblo's remarkable aspen-lined Santa Clara Canyon to visit the Puyé Cliff Dwelling ruins, which are part of the pueblo. There are also exhibits of the pueblo's pottery, which features blackware, redware, and a technique called sgraffito. The canyon area includes campsites, picnic settings, and hiking trails.

Nambé Pueblo (all ages)
Highway 503 off US 285/84, between Santa Fe and Española; (505) 455–2036.

In Tewa, Nambé means "Pueblo of the Roundish Ruins." The friendly Nambé have opened their reservation for tourists to enjoy.

They offer hiking trails that will take you and your kids to the beautiful double-drop waterfall. You can swim in the pools around the waterfall, camp along the Rio Nambé, and get some trout fishing in, too. There's also a herd of buffalo that you can see by contacting the pueblo's buffalo keeper. A good time to visit is the Fourth of July, when the pueblo presents its annual Nambé Falls Ceremonial. Your kids will get to see a variety of ceremonial dances, many of them performed by the children of the tribes that participate in this mini-powwow.

Where to Eat

Dos Amigos Cafe. 1213 North Riverside Drive; (505) 753–3161. Popular spot for classic northern New Mexican food. Open daily 6:00 A.M. to 10:00 P.M. $–$$

El Paragua. Corner of Highway 76 and Highway 68; (505) 753–3211. One of the best Mexican restaurants in northern New Mexico. Outdoor dining. Mariachi music on the weekends. Open 11:00 A.M. to 9:00 P.M. $–$$

Flavios Cafe. 230 Oñate NW; (505) 753–6127. Creative and tasty Mexican and American food in a casual atmosphere. Open 11:00 A.M. to 3:00 P.M. $–$$

Where to Stay

Comfort Inn. 604 South Riverside Drive; (505) 753–2419. Forty-one rooms, cable television, hot tub. Restaurant nearby. $$

Inn at the Delta. 304 Paseo de Oñate Drive; (505) 753–9466 or (800) 995–8599; www.innatthedelta.com. Ten rooms (some with whirlpools and fireplaces) fill the adobe building. Children under 12 **free.** Complimentary full breakfast; very good restaurant on premises (Anthony's). $$–$$$

Super 8 Motel. 811 South Riverside Drive; (505) 753–5374. This motel offers 50 rooms and a restaurant nearby. Cable television, too. $–$$

For More Information

Chamber of Commerce. (505) 753–2831; espanola.com/chamber.

Abiquiu

US 84, 15 miles from Española.

This village is known as the place where the famous artist Georgia O'Keeffe lived and worked. The little town itself has a charming church that was refurbished about fifteen years ago and is another lovely example of adobe architecture.

The Home of Georgia O'Keeffe (ages 10 to 12)
From Española, go north on US 84 to Abiquiu via Chama (22 miles). House is on the left just before the village, opposite the Abiquiu Inn; (505) 685–4539. Tours April through November by reservation only. Make your reservations well in advance, especially during the summer. Admission: $22 for adults, $17 for students and seniors.

Until quite recently, the guardian of O'Keeffe's estate refused to allow visitors on the grounds of her home, but now visitors can look around the house where O'Keeffe worked and lived. Some of her art hangs on the walls, which your children will find interesting.

Ghost Ranch Living Museum and Conference Center (ages 10 to 12)
US 84, 12 miles north of Abiquiu; (505) 685–4333. Open Tuesday through Sunday 9:00 A.M. to 5:00 P.M. Admission: by donation.

The museum lets the kids look through telescopes, climb a forest ranger lookout tower, and watch the indoor/outdoor beaver hatch. It also explains the 12,000-year history and paleontology of the area and has a collection of contemporary art. On the east side of the road leading to Ghost Ranch is part of the set where *City Slickers* was filmed.

Florence Hawley Ellis Museum of Anthropology (all ages)
At Ghost Ranch on US 84; (505) 685–4333.

Ghost Ranch also has this interesting museum, which displays the artifacts of civilizations that inhabited the area over the last 12,000 years. In 1947 a mass burial site of dinosaurs was discovered nearby, so there's also an exhibit of the Coelophysis (pronounced see-low-FY-sis) dinosaur for the kids to study.

Echo Amphitheater (all ages)
US 84, 35 miles from Española. Open year-round. **Free.**

This natural outcropping of huge red rocks will delight the kids. Here they can stand in the middle, give a big "Whoop!" and hear their own voices repeat and repeat as the sound bounces from one rock to another. This makes a great stop for everyone to rest and enjoy a picnic and the gorgeous surroundings. Camping is **free,** and there are toilets, grills, garbage pickups, and tables at or near the sites.

Abiquiu Lake (all ages)
US 84, 7 miles northwest of Abiquiu; (505) 685–4371. Open year-round. **Free.**

Two boat ramps are located at the north end, along with showers and grills. Most people swim near the boat ramps.

Poshouinge Ruins (ages 10 to 12)
US 84 north, just past Highway 554 to the west. Open year-round. **Free.**

The trail is just a ½ mile and traverses some steep and uneven terrain. There are interpretive signs along the way and two gorgeous views of the Chama River Valley. It is pronounced "Po-SU-in-geh."

Where to Eat

Bode's General Store. Highway 84; (505) 685–4422. Great deli items and sandwiches—the perfect place to pick up food for a picnic lunch. Open Friday, Saturday, and Sunday 7:00 A.M. to 8:00 P.M., rest of week 6:00 A.M. to 7:00 P.M. $

Where to Stay

Abiquiu Inn. Highway 84; (505) 685–4378 or (800) 447–5621; www.abiquiuinn.com.

Nineteen lovely rooms, some with private veranda and fireplace fill the inn. Restaurant features freshly prepared food with a Southwestern touch. Gallery and gift shop on site. $$–$$$

For More Information

State of New Mexico Tourist Office. (800) 733–6396; www.newmexico.org.

Chama

US 84, 90 miles north of Española.

Chama offers you and your family a great opportunity to see some wonderful scenery and visit one or two historic areas in this part of New Mexico. It is located about 8,000 feet above sea level. This is an area that gets a tremendous amount of snow and has wondrous cross-country skiing trails. The summer is perhaps the best and safest time to visit this popular town near the Colorado border.

Cumbres & Toltec Scenic Railroad (all ages)

Depot located 1½ miles inside Chama opposite the Cumbres Mall on the 400 block of Terrace Road; (505) 756–2151 or (888) 286–2737; www.cumbrestoltec.com. Open mid-May through October. Ticket prices for coach seating range from $37.00 to $69.75. Reservations are recommended.

You and your children will love this excursion. The hundred-year-old train was built originally to transport the ore out of the nearby Colorado mines; now it is a tourist attraction. The 64-mile narrow gauge rail is the longest in the United States and the highest, since it chugs through the Cumbres Pass at more than 10,000 feet. Because you are so high, it will be chilly even in the summertime, so dress warmly and bring lots of water. As you and the kids ride the rails, you'll edge along the 1,000-foot-deep gorge and travel through a 366-foot-long tunnel carved out of solid rock and an astonishing 349-foot-long mud and wood tunnel. The kids will never forget this ride as they cross and recross the New Mexico and Colorado borders eleven times. The train does stop for lunch at a hamlet called Osier. You can purchase something here, or bring a picnic along with you.

Humphries State Wildlife Area (all ages)

US 84/64, 10 miles southwest of Chama before Dulce city limits. Contact Department of Game and Fish: (505) 841–8881. Admission: $5.00 for day use, $10.00 for an overnight stay at a developed site ($8.00 for undeveloped). Extra for hookups and sewage facilities.

The park's 9,000 acres are full of elk. You can ride horses into the elk habitat or hike in. Campsites are also available.

Christ in the **Desert Monastery**

Forest Service Road 151, 13 miles west of US 84 north of Ghost Ranch.

Visiting this Benedictine monastery on the way back to Española is not essential, but it is certainly gorgeous. It is extremely isolated along a difficult, unpaved road. If there is rain or snow, the only kind of vehicle that can make it there is a sturdy 4x4. Visiting here is primarily suitable for children 10 or older, and pets are not allowed (neither is revealing, casual summer wear like shorts). Despite these constraints, you won't regret walking the grounds of this peaceful place. The monastery is a religious house of contemplation, so you won't see monks strolling around, greeting you; they are engaged in their spiritual life. You're on the honor system of behavior, even when making a purchase from the gift shop. You'll find a chapel open to the general public and some of the loveliest countryside in northern New Mexico. Reservations are not required (there aren't any telephones, anyway).

Heron Lake and El Vado Lake State Parks (all ages)

Heron Lake is 8 miles west of Tierra Amarilla on Highway 95 via US 64; (505) 588–7470. El Vado is 18 miles southwest of Tierra Amarilla on Highway 112; (505) 588–7247. Heron Lake has a visitor center. Hookups, showers, and campgrounds at both. Admission: $5.00 for day use, $8.00 for a primitive campsite, $10.00 for a developed campsite ($4.00 for hookups).

The area of these twin lakes was explored by Franciscan friars scouting new territories to establish churches. The lakes offer some wonderful fishing for you and your family—Kokanee salmon, channel catfish, and both rainbow and brown trout. The lakes also serve as a bird sanctuary. If your kids have keen eyesight and a good birding book, they may be able to spot red-tailed hawks, osprey, Clark's nutcrackers, and hairy woodpeckers. The bald eagle considers this state park its wintering ground. There isn't a public marina, but you can rent pontoon boats, pedal boats, canoes, and fishing boats at Stone House Lodge on Heron Lake Road (Highway 95; 505–588–7274). There is a 5½-mile connecting trail along the Rio Chama.

Old Town **Visits**

While you and the kids are driving around this area, consider visiting three other very small but old towns: **Los Ojos** ("The Eyes"), 10 miles south of Chama on Highway 95 west; **La Puente** ("The Bridge"), 5 miles farther south on Highway 95; and **Los Brazos** ("The Arms"), 8 miles from Chama along Highway 512 east. All three are considered the oldest villages in the Chama Valley, with more than half the houses in them deemed "significant structures" by the state and federal registers of historic places. You and your family can get a delightful peek at the unique architecture of these old homes with their blend of adobe and European/Victorian details.

Where to Eat

High Country Restaurant. Main Street in town; (505) 756–2384. Comfortable eatery with good sandwiches, seafood, and chicken. Children's menu. Open daily 11:00 A.M. to 10:00 P.M. $–$$

Jennifer's. Highway 17; (505) 756–1956. American and Mexican drive-through. Open daily 9:00 A.M. to 7:00 P.M. $

Patsy's Restaurant and Bakery. 1810 South Highway 17; (505) 756–2108. Open Monday through Friday 11:00 A.M. to 7:00 P.M. $–$$

Where to Stay

Branding Iron Motel. US 84; (505) 756–2162 or (800) 446–2650. Located in town, with a restaurant on premises, laundry nearby. Thirty-nine well-maintained, oversize rooms offer cable television and free coffee. $–$$

Elk Horn Lodge. 2 miles south on Route 1 off US 84; (505) 756–2105 or (800) 532–8874. The lodge has twenty-two rooms; eleven cabins (sleeping two to eight people) with kitchenettes. Heated pool, cable television, and phones. Located on the banks of the Chama River. Fishing allowed (with a license) in the rainbow trout–stocked river. Pets welcome ($10.00 per night). $$–$$$

For More Information

Visitor Information Center. 2372 Highway 17; (505) 756–2235.

Chamber of Commerce. (505) 756–2306 or (800) 477–0149; www.chamavalley.com.

Annual Community Events

LATE FEBRUARY–EARLY MARCH
Chama Winter Carnival. Locations vary every year; (505) 756–2306 or (800) 477–0149. Balloon rally, dancing and music, and Nordic ski competitions.

JULY
Chama Valley Music Festival. Community Center, 393 Fourth Street (at Terrace Avenue, or Highway 17); (505) 756–2306 or (800) 477–0149. Series of concerts over a three-week period featuring a range of styles, from jug bands to big band to classical. Children are welcome. Tickets are reasonably priced.

EARLY AUGUST
Chama Days. Rodeo grounds (off Highway 17); (505) 756–2306 or (800) 477–0149. Rodeo, parade, art show, music, and dances.

Los Alamos

US 285/84 to Highway 502 for 18 miles.

People who visit this world-famous town come either admiring it or despising it. Here is where the greatest scientists of their time gathered in the 1940s to create the atomic bomb. Nobel Prize-winning physicists Enrico Fermi and Niels Bohr and nuclear physicist J. Robert Oppenheimer all lived on this mesa, called the Pajarito ("little bird") Plateau, high in the mountains surrounding Santa Fe. They operated in the utmost secrecy—there wasn't even a mailing address for them. Their task was to work on what the government called The Manhattan Project, which ultimately produced the bombs that were dropped on Hiroshima and Nagasaki, Japan. Los Alamos is small and almost a time warp of a per-fectly preserved town of the 1950s. White Rock is the suburb where the people who work in Los Alamos live.

Bradbury Science Museum (ages 10 to 12) 🏛

Fifteenth Street and Central Avenue; (505) 667–4444. Open Tuesday through Friday 9:00 A.M. to 5:00 P.M., Saturday through Monday 1:00 to 5:00 P.M. Free.

My son called this place the "Milton Bradley Museum" for years. Even though there are no board games here, a visit to this intelligent and well-displayed museum is an important stop for your family to gain an insight into a significant moment in American history. There are several hands-on displays for the kids to get involved with, as well as replicas of the test bombs, Little Boy and Fat Man, and an interesting short film describing the life and times of the era.

Los Alamos Historical Museum (ages 10 to 12)

1921 Juniper Street; (505) 662–6272; www.losalamos.com/historicalsociety/museum.asp. Open Monday through Saturday 9:30 A.M. to 4:30 P.M., Sunday 11:00 A.M. to 5:00 P.M. Admission: Free.

Before the town was used as a war laboratory, it served as a school for boys suffering from various illnesses. All of the kids lived in a huge two-story, log-cabin building called the Fuller Lodge. When the government decided to use the town for its atomic research, they sent the boys home and used the lodge to house the scientists. This museum is on the grounds of the Fuller Lodge. You and the children will enjoy the exhibits that range from a look at the earliest inhabitants of the plateau to a peek into the living room and kitchen of a typical World War II housing facility. You can also wander through the lodge itself and imagine what it must have been like all those years ago in an atmosphere of secrecy and war.

Otowi Station Science Museum Shop (all ages)

1350 Central Avenue; (505) 662–9589. Open Monday through Friday 8:00 A.M. to 8:00 P.M., Saturday 9:00 A.M. to 6:00 P.M., Sunday 11:00 A.M. to 6:00 P.M.

This is a great place to stop for science kits, puzzles, and special educational books and toys from around the world. There are also lots of special activities for kids (usually on weekends).

White Rock Overlook Park (all ages)

Highway 502 to Highway 4 to White Rock. Take Rover Boulevard to the first traffic light, then second left onto Meadow for 10 blocks through a residential area, then third left onto Overlook Road. Go all the way (past the baseball field) to the end of the road. Free.

This side trip is well worth the bit of meandering you do to get to the park. It offers a striking view of the Rio Grande Canyon. Take the rim trail around it, and imagine when the whole area was underwater and the volcanoes were erupting.

Bandelier National Monument (all ages)

Highway 501 out of Los Alamos to Highway 4 south for 13 miles; (505) 672–3861; www.nps.gov/band. Open daily from 8:00 A.M. to 4:30 P.M. in the winter, longer hours rest of year. Admission: $10 per car.

This 23,000-acre area is one of the largest archaeological sites in New Mexico and perhaps in the Southwest. The children will love visiting Frijoles ("Beans") Canyon and climbing the ladders to the cliff dwellings notched into the canyon walls. The monument is full of hiking trails, historic sites, and woodlands. A stop at the visitor center is a must for detailed maps and age-appropriate ideas for a day trip. For older children, there is the Falls Trail (my personal favorite), a 5-mile round-trip from the parking lot to the Rio Grande. It is varied enough that you get a bit of everything the park has to offer. Another excursion, this one centered on the earlier inhabitants of the area, is the Ceremonial Cave. You have to climb four steep and arduous ladders to reach the cave, 140 feet up. For those

State **Cookie**

The state cookie is the *bizcochito*, a sweet flaky biscuit to which a bit of anise has been added.

with younger children, there is a paved mile-long loop path that gets you and the kids to the great views. You can camp here and explore the backcountry, too. Permits, available at the monument's entrance, are required for both. There are also candlelight tours of the ruins in the summer and winter. Wear layered clothing and sturdy hiking shoes, and carry lots of water, snacks, and sunscreen.

San Ildefonso Pueblo (all ages)
US 84/285 to Highway 502, heading to Los Alamos, 24 miles north of Santa Fe; (505) 455–3549.

The first thing your kids will notice is the large black outcropping known as the Black Mesa. Historically, this is where Indian warriors fought off the Spanish invaders. But legends tell of a giant who once lived on top of the mesa and ate naughty boys and girls who wandered too far off the pueblo. San Ildefonso is small but delightful and is well known for the pottery created by Maria Martinez. Her work is in museums around the world. There's a well-stocked fishing lake and a modest museum that will help the children understand the life and culture of the tribe.

Tsankawi **Ruins**

Highway 502 to Highway 4 for a ½ mile, parking lot is on your left before first traffic light; (505) 672–3861. Open from dawn to dusk. Admission: $10 per car.

This is my favorite part of Bandelier National Monument. For most of this 1½-mile trail, you walk the edge of a mesa. You are as high as the crows that fly by, and the vistas are incredible (there is no better view of Black Mesa). Much of the rock in the trail has been worn away over time. My son likes to raise dust storms in the caves while I try to find and interpret the petroglyphs on the walls. There is a self-guided tour map available in the parking lot. There are portable toilets but no drinking water. Be careful with young children; there are no fences or guardrails along the edge.

Where to Eat

Central Avenue Grill. 1789 Central Avenue; (505) 662–2005. Sandwiches, soups, and salads. Open Monday through Friday 11:00 A.M. to 8:30 P.M., and Saturday for dinner only, 5:00 to 9:00 P.M. $$

China Moon. 121 Central Park Square; (505) 662–2883. Chinese food. Open daily 11:00 A.M. to 9:00 P.M. $–$$

Tony's Pizza. 723 Central Avenue; (505) 662–7799. Pizza and pasta. Open daily 11:00 A.M. to 8:00 P.M. $–$$

Where to Stay

Best Western Hilltop. 400 Trinity Drive; (505) 662–2441. All ninety-two rooms (some suites) have beautiful views. Offers continental breakfast, bar, laundry on site. Children under 12 **free.**

Hampton Inn and Suites. 132 Highway 4, White Rock; (505) 672–3838. Playground, dry-heat sauna, laundry facilities, complimentary full breakfast. All seventy-two rooms have microwave and refrigerator, some have kitchenettes. $–$$

Los Alamos Inn. 2201 Trinity Drive; (505) 662–7211. 116 rooms. Brand-new upscale nightclub/restaurant with entertainment on premises. Small pets welcome at no charge. $$

For More Information

Chamber of Commerce. (505) 662–8105; www.visit.losalamos.com.

Other **Attractions**

- **Los Alamos Aquatic Center.** 2760 Canyon Road; (505) 662–8170. Open Monday through Friday 6:00 A.M. to 8:00 P.M. and Saturday 10:00 A.M. to 5:00 P.M. Admission: $3.25 for adults, $2.00 for seniors and children under 17. A high-altitude, Olympic-size pool and a therapy pool.

- **Los Alamos Ice Rink.** 4250 Diamond Drive; (505) 662–4500. The only outdoor ice rink in northern New Mexico also is open in the summer for in-line skating. Call for prices.

- **Pajarito Mountain Ski Area.** NM 501/West Jémez Road; (505) 662–5725 or (505) 662–SNOW; www.skipajarito.com. This is where serious skiers go to escape the crowds during the busy season.

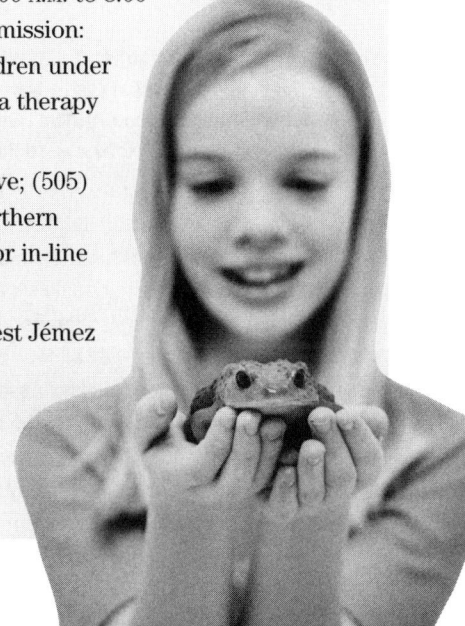

For Further **Reference**

The Woman at Otowi Crossing by Frank Waters (Swallow Books). This is a fictionalized account of the life of Edith Warner, who ran a tea room at the edge of the Rio Grande where the Los Alamos scientists and members of the neighboring pueblos would visit.

Santa Fe

I–25 north at US 285/84 exit (St. Francis Drive).

Santa Fe was founded in 1607 by Don Pedro de Peralta on the site of an ancient Tanoan Indian village. Although it is a small state capital, with only 62,000 inhabitants, it is the oldest, and because of the diversity of its people and their cultures, it is considered an international city. Once in Santa Fe, there's no end of things to do.

Santa Fe Plaza (all ages)

This should be your first stop. Featured in just about every magazine article on New Mexico, the plaza is a vivid, colorful crossroads and represents almost four centuries of local civilization. About 150 years ago, it was the end of the line for the covered wagon caravans using the Santa Fe Trail, a dusty, cluttered depot for traders and cowboys. Now there are gift shops, restaurants, and museums surrounding the grassy center.

Museum of New Mexico (ages 10 to 12)

725 Camino Lejo; (505) 476–1125 or (505) 827–6463; www.museumofnewmexico.org. The museums are open Tuesday through Sunday 10:00 A.M. to 5:00 P.M.

This is an organization operated by the state that oversees four of the major museums in Santa Fe (the Palace of the Governors, Museum of Fine Arts, Museum of Indian Arts and Culture, and Museum of International Folk Art) and five historic monuments in the state. It also sponsors research, education, and conservation. You can visit all four of the museums for a reduced rate ($15.00 for a four-day pass per person age 17 and older; children 16 and under get in **free**); otherwise, it is $7.00 per visit, per day (tickets can be obtained at any of the museums or monuments). You may want to visit or call to see if this is a good offer for your family.

Palace of the Governors (ages 10 to 12)
West side of Santa Fe Plaza on Palace between Lincoln and Washington; (505) 476–5100.

Under the portal of the 370-year-old Palace of the Governors, the kids will be amazed to see Native Americans from the surrounding pueblos selling their wares. The palace itself is an interesting museum chronicling the history of New Mexico's capital city, the oldest continually used seat of government in the country. Several of the rooms are furnished as in a Spanish colonial house. In the courtyard the kids can take a look at a real covered wagon.

Museum of Fine Arts (ages 10 to 12)
107 West Palace Avenue; (505) 476–5072. Open Tuesday through Sunday 10:00 A.M. to 5:00 P.M., Friday to 8:00 P.M. Admission: Free from 5:00 to 8:00 P.M.

This museum showcases some of the best painted and sculpted works from New Mexico artists, past and present. The museum's St. Francis Auditorium also houses many concerts of the Santa Fe Chamber Music Festival during the summer.

Museum of Indian Arts and Culture (ages 10 to 12)
708 Camino Lejo (off Old Santa Fe Trail); (505) 476–1250; www.miaclab.org. Open Tuesday through Sunday 10:00 A.M. to 5:00 P.M.

Here your kids will learn more about the various Native American cultures that have existed in New Mexico for thousands of years. The museum offers classes for both children and adults on such subjects as Navajo basketry, pueblo foods, and Cochiti drum-making.

Historic **Walking Tours**

Every day except Sunday, from mid-May through mid-October; (505) 476–5100.

This tour of the city is sponsored by the Palace of the Governors. They are accurate, fresh, and colorful excursions led by highly trained, knowledgeable docents. Most of these circuits last about ninety minutes and are not too tiring even for younger children. So much history has been lived in Santa Fe that even kids who seem uninterested in buildings and facts will be taken with these walks. An extra benefit here is that when you buy a ticket, you are also helping to support historic preservation of the important buildings of New Mexico.

Tesuque

North of Santa Fe (either heading out 5 miles on Highway 285/84 or taking the more scenic route from Bishop's Lodge Road) is the village of Tesuque, which shares its name with the nearby pueblo. The two big draws in town are the **Shidoni Foundry** (505–988–8001) with its beautiful bronze sculpture gardens, and the **Tesuque Village Market** (505–988–8848), which is a lovely place to have a great meal and watch for the celebrities who live in the area.

Museum of International Folk Art (all ages)

706 Camino Lejo (off Old Santa Fe Trail); (505) 476–1200; www.moifa.org. Open Tuesday through Sunday 10:00 A.M. to 5:00 P.M.

This museum has one of the best collections of folk art in the world, and your children will enjoy the exhibits. The main collection of toys and artifacts from around the world is especially fascinating. There are often weekend classes or special exhibits highlighting crafts or food specialties, as well as traveling exhibits. The Museum Hill Cafe, featuring good lunch food, is within walking distance of this museum and the Museum of Indian Arts and Culture.

Georgia O'Keeffe Museum (ages 10 to 12)

217 Johnson Street; (505) 995–0785; www.okeeffemuseum.org. Open daily 10:00 A.M. to 5:00 P.M. Admission: $8.00 for adults, $7.00 for seniors, children under 16 free. Admission is free Fridays from 5:00 to 8:00 P.M.

The only museum dedicated to a female artist, it highlights the work of all the periods of O'Keeffe's life.

La Fonda Hotel (ages 10 to 12)

100 East San Francisco Street; (505) 982–5511.

This is the original Harvey Hotel that marked the end of the Santa Fe Trail, where cowboys, traders, and celebrities have stayed. It was the first destination for the Los Alamos scientists, and, supposedly, Billy the Kid washed dishes in the kitchen way back when. Take the kids inside to check out the dining room, which is surrounded by small-paned windows all hand-painted with delightful drawings of fruit, flowers, birds, and other designs. It's amazing.

St. Francis Cathedral (all ages)

131 Cathedral Place, at the end of San Francisco Street. Parish office: (505) 982–5619. Call for schedules of masses; you can usually visit the cathedral between them if you don't want to attend.

The cathedral was built in 1869 under the direction of the first archbishop of Santa Fe, Jean-Baptiste Lamy. Whether or not you are Catholic, you might want to take the children to the 8:00 A.M. Sunday Mass, which is conducted in Spanish and features a mariachi band and a Spanish choir. Your whole family will be impressed by the vividness of this service.

Loretto Chapel (all ages)
207 Old Santa Fe Trail, south of Water Street; (505) 982–0092; www.lorettochapel.com. Open Monday through Saturday 9:00 A.M. to 6:00 P.M., Sunday 10:30 A.M. to 5:00 P.M. Admission: $2.50 for adults, children under 7 free.

This was once the chapel for the convent attached to St. Francis Cathedral. There is a fanciful legend about the beautifully curved staircase that you'll see at the back of this charming French-style chapel: An old German craftsman answered the prayers of the nuns when

Rancho de las Golondrinas

I–25 at exit 276 to 334 Los Pinos Road, 15 miles southwest of Santa Fe; (505) 471–2261; www.golondrinas.org. Open June through October, Wednesday through Sunday 10:00 A.M. to 4:00 P.M. Self-guided tours are $5.00 for adults, $4.00 for seniors and children 13–18, $2.00 for children 5–12. Additional fees for special events and guided tours.

This is a delightful eighteenth-century working museum that marks the end of the Camino Real, which started in Chihuahua, Mexico. The "Ranch of the Barn Swallows" is a must-see for both you and the kids, especially if you select one of the festival weekends that the ranch sponsors during the summer. In early May there is a Civil War weekend featuring a reenactment of the battle at Glorieta Pass, a colorful event that the kids will enjoy. Even if your trip doesn't coincide with one of these times, your kids can still see bread baking in the *hornos*, watch the Spanish and Roman-style molinas (flour mills) grinding wheat and corn, and walk to the beautifully restored rooms and houses on this 300-acre walled ranch. Be sure to stop at the pigpen in the Sierra Village area of the museum; this was a location for the films *Young Guns* and *Wyatt Earp*. There are knowledgeable guides who are available to answer any questions you may have. The museum has an excellent gift shop full of authentic reproductions of everything from toys to tinware for your table. There's also a great selection of children's books about this era.

they realized that the chapel had been built without a staircase. He quoted them an amazingly fair price, they hired him, and the very next morning, when they filed in for prayers, there was the staircase as you see it today. The kids will get a kick out of the story, and you'll enjoy the charm of the tiny church's architecture. There are often concerts given here; check with the information desk. Also, check out "Footsteps across New Mexico," a thirty-minute multimedia presentation on the history of New Mexico.

Santuario de Guadalupe (all ages)
100 Guadalupe at Agua Fria; (505) 988–2027. Open Monday through Saturday 9:00 A.M. to 4:00 P.M. Donations requested.

This is considered by many experts to be the oldest mission church in the United States. The kids should keep their eyes out for the banners on the wall that have the image of Our Lady of Guadalupe. They are very old and made of animal hides. The banners were used by the Spanish missionaries to teach the Native Americans about Christianity.

Institute of American Indian Arts Museum (ages 10 to 12)
108 Cathedral Place at Palace Avenue and San Francisco Street (across from the cathedral); (505) 983–1777 or (505) 983–8900; www.iaiancad.org. Open Monday through Saturday 9:00 A.M. to 5:00 P.M., Sunday 10:00 A.M. to 5:00 P.M. Admission: $4.00 for adults, seniors, and students over 16, $2.00 for children 16 years and younger.

While much of the knowledge we have about Native Americans of the Southwest focuses on their ancient arts and artifacts, this museum displays contemporary Indian talent. Some of the exhibitions are whole environments with which you and your children can interact. **Note:** At press time the museum was closed for renovations through spring 2005. Call first before visiting.

Canyon Road (ages 10 to 12)
Just past Paseo de Peralta and Alameda.

This world-famous street of art galleries and shops used to be an Indian trail leading (eventually) to the Pecos Pueblo. It can be fun to stroll along it if only to people-watch and glance at the colorful windows full of the art that makes this area so well known. One of the best times to visit is on Friday evenings, when the galleries launch their new exhibits.

Horseback Riding **in Santa Fe**

- **Bishop's Lodge.** 3 miles north of the plaza; (505) 983–6377 or (800) 732–2240. Full- or half-day trail rides in the Sangre de Cristo Mountains.
- **Broken Saddle Riding Company.** Cerrillos (15 miles south of Santa Fe); (505) 470–0074. Ride the Turquoise Trail.
- The visitor bureau has more suggestions.

New Mexico **State Flag**

The current state flag was designed and approved in 1925. The red design that you see decorating the yellow flag (the two favorite colors of Queen Isabella of Spain) is the sacred symbol of the Zia Pueblo. Four is their sacred number, representing the four directions, the four stages in a day, in a year, and in a life, and the four duties: a strong body, a clear mind, a pure spirit, and a devotion to others. The circle demonstrates the life and love flowing through these multiple fours that are without beginning or end. Lately, the Zia Pueblo is protesting its use and asking for compensation.

The whole area is out for an amble. Exotic-art collectors, students, and locals enjoy both the pictures and the **free** snacks that the galleries offer to their customers and browsers. The artists themselves are usually on the scene, willing to discuss their works with you and your family.

State Capitol, The Roundhouse (ages 10 to 12)
Paseo de Peralta at Old Santa Fe Trail (parking on Old Santa Fe Trail).

The capitol was designed to resemble a Navajo hogan. Several of the sculptures outside have been made by internationally recognized local artists such as Glenna Goodacre. Inside, the building is full of the best art around. Each piece is well annotated. The legislative session runs from January to March, and you can sit in the gallery of either house and see bills debated firsthand.

Santa Fe Children's Museum (all ages)
1050 Old Pecos Trail; (505) 989–8359; www.santafechildrensmuseum.org. Open Wednesday through Saturday 10:00 A.M. to 5:00 P.M., Sunday noon to 5:00 P.M. Admission: $4.00 for adults and children.

The hands-on museum features innumerable exhibits designed for children. There are visiting artists, water-play, snakes, bubble-making, face-painting, and especially interesting ways of illustrating science concepts in fun ways. My son and I spent most of his early childhood here.

For Further **Reference**

Santa Fe on Foot: Adventures in the City Different by Elaine Pinkerton Coleman (Ocean Tree Books).

Santa Fe **Detours**

107 Washington Avenue or 54½ East San Francisco Street; (505) 983–6565 or (800) DETOURS. Walking tours, horseback riding excursions, rafting, and other "Southwest Safaris," as well as accommodations.

Wheelwright Museum (ages 10 to 12)
704 Camino Lejo; (505) 982–4636; www.wheelwright.org. Open Monday through Saturday 10:00 A.M. to 5:00 P.M., Sunday 1:00 to 5:00 P.M. Free (donations appreciated).

Shaped like a hogan, this unique museum specializes in contemporary Native American art. It does not fall under the umbrella of the Museum of New Mexico. Downstairs, there's a replica of a genuine trading post full of some beautiful jewelry and artifacts of the Native tribes in the area. There are also plenty of trinkets and books that the kids will like.

Randall Davey Audubon Center (all ages)
Top of Upper Canyon Road (take Canyon Road to Alameda, turn right, then take the first left); (505) 983–4609. Trails are open daily from 9:00 A.M. to 5:00 P.M. (Visitor center open to 4:00 P.M.) Admission: $2.00 for adults, $1.00 for children 12 and under.

This is great place to get away from the hubbub without straying too far from it all. The center is a nature sanctuary operated by the Audubon Society. There are numerous, easy trails and the chance for some beautiful views of the flora and fauna that flourish here. In the summertime, there's a wonderful half-day camp for kids that you can do for a week or a day. The classes cover mapmaking and compass reading, tracking and rock identification. The center also offers study walks and regular tours of the Davey House.

Turquoise **Trail**

Highway 14 and the National Scenic Byway (Highway 536). This is a more scenic and adventurous alternative to the drive between Santa Fe and Albuquerque. The route takes you through Cerrillos, Madrid, and Golden, three old mining towns that are coming alive again as art communities.

Rafting in **Santa Fe**

Both of the following outfits offer full- and half-day trips on the Rio Grande.

- **New Wave Rafting** (505) 984–1444 or (800) 984–1444; www.newwave rafting.com
- **Santa Fe Rafting Co.** (505) 988–4914 or (800) 467–RAFT

Planetarium (all ages)

On the campus of Santa Fe Community College at the end of Richards Avenue; (505) 428–1677 (reservations). Admission varies per event.

This place can be a lot of fun for the whole family. There are wonderful astronomy classes for the kids, and programs take place regularly on Thursday nights.

Cochiti Pueblo (all ages)

I–25 south to exit 259. Take Highway 16 to the pueblo; (505) 465–2244.

Cochiti Pueblo is famous for the storyteller dolls that you'll see in every gift shop from Albuquerque to Taos. The figurine, a seated woman covered with frolicking children, was invented in 1964 by Pueblo native Helen Cordero. Cochiti's other, more ancient fame rests on the deep-toned ceremonial drums certain tribesmen make by hand.

Cochiti Lake (all ages)

Take I–25 to exit 259 (at the bottom of La Bajada Hill), then west on Highway 16 for about 8 miles. (505) 465–2300 (Cochiti Ranger Station). Open year-round. Free.

The U.S. Army Corps of Engineers administers this man-made lake. You and the kids can enjoy camping, swimming, sailing, and boating. I even learned how to windsurf here. The lake is stocked with trout, bass, and northern pike. In the camping area there are RV hookups, a snack bar, a swimming pool, a Laundromat, and a small general store.

Farmers' **Market**

Guadalupe Street and Cerrillos Road, at the Santa Fe Railyard, behind SITE Santa Fe; (505) 983–4098 or (888) 983–4400.

Farmers from 50 miles around bring their produce and homemade food to sell on Tuesday and Saturday mornings. It is a very happy place to be on a beautiful Santa Fe morning. Open from May to November.

Santa Fe **Ski Area**

End of Hyde Park Road (which starts out as Artist's Road, 1 block north of Paseo de Peralta on Bishop's Lodge Road); (505) 982–4429; snow phone (505) 983–9155; www.skisantafe.com. Offers a little bit for everyone, from Thanksgiving to Easter (weather permitting). Check out the children's Adventureland.

Tetilla Peak Campgrounds (all ages)

From Highway 16 (exit 259 off I–25), take La Bajada (turn right) and go for 11 miles to the peak; (505) 465–0274. Developed campgrounds are $11.00 Monday through Thursday, $12.00 Friday through Sunday. Undeveloped sites are $7.00 and $8.00, respectively. Showers, shelters, and a dump station. No RV hookups.

Tetilla Peak is a beautiful mountain overlooking Cochiti Lake known for its spectacular vistas. It is open only from April through October.

Kasha-Katuwe Tent Rocks National Monument (all ages)

Take Highway 16 from exit 259 off I–25 and follow it all the way to the Cochiti Pueblo, bearing left as you pass the dam. The entrance to the park is ¼ mile on the right after the pueblo (there is a 6-mile rough dirt road to the entrance). (505) 465–2244. Open daily, sunrise to sunset. There is an admission charge per vehicle, posted at parking area.

By far the most exciting experience for the kids in this area is a hike through this park. Here the ancient rocks have been shaped by centuries of wind and rain into mysterious tentlike objects with "balls" on top. The hiking is unforgettable as you twist your way through narrow canyons of rock that lead to lovely vistas of juniper and more gorgeous rock formations. As the sun and clouds play across the landscape, the colors and contours change and change again. This is not a climb for strollers or baby backpacks, because of the tight passages through the rocks and the degree of climbing you'll have to do. Bring a picnic, sturdy shoes, and plenty of water. This is an out-of-the-way, rugged area.

Dixon Apple Farm (all ages)

Highway 16 to Highway 22 west to Peña Blanca; (505) 465–2976. Open daily from 8:00 A.M. to 5:00 P.M. during harvest season in mid-September. As the season's actual dates change each year, call before heading out to the farm.

The farm is famous for its apples found only here: the Sparkling Burgundy and the Champagne. You and the kids can visit any time of the year and enjoy the delights of the farm. The best time to go, of course, is during harvesttime, from mid-September into October. Then you can eat the apples, enjoy Dixon's acclaimed cider, and have a picnic lunch on the grounds.

Oldest House **in Santa Fe**

215 East DeVargas Street. On a map from 1882, this property was labeled "the oldest house in Santa Fe." There is evidence of a similar structure in an earlier (1760) map, and specimens taken from the house's *vigas* seem to confirm its age.

Where to Eat

Cowgirl Hall of Fame. 319 South Guadalupe Street; (505) 982–2565; www.cowgirlsantafe.com. Everything from barbecue to filet mignon, plus a kids' menu and play area. Open Monday through Friday 11:00 A.M. to 11:00 P.M., Saturday and Sunday 8:30 A.M. to 11:00 P.M. $$

The Plaza Restaurant. Lincoln Avenue, on the west side of Santa Fe Plaza; (505) 982–1664. Cozy but lively diner on the plaza. Mexican, American, and Greek food. Children's menu. Open daily 7:00 A.M. to 9:00 P.M. $–$$

The Tecolote. 1203 Cerrillos Road; (505) 988–1362. Specializes in breakfast dishes. Children's menu. Open 7:00 A.M. to 2:00 P.M. $–$$

Zia Diner. 326 Guadalupe Street; (505) 988–7008. Local favorite for really good, inexpensive fare. They welcome children. Open daily 7:00 A.M. to 10:00 P.M. $–$$

Where to Stay

Bishop's Lodge. Bishop's Lodge Road, 3 miles north of the plaza; (800) 732–2240; www.bishopslodge.com. A former girls' boarding school, the 111-room guest ranch offers horseback riding, hiking trails, tennis courts, and swimming. $$$

El Rey Inn. 1862 Cerrillos Road; (505) 982–1931; www.elreysantafe.com. This 1935 Spanish hacienda-style motel is one of the three oldest establishments in Santa Fe. The eighty-six rooms are all different and range from the simple to the luxurious. Some have balconies, patios, fireplaces, and kitchens. Playground, outdoor heated pool, hot tubs, and laundry facilities. Complimentary continental breakfast. Sorry, no pets. $$–$$$

Holiday Inn Express. 3470 Cerrillos Road; (505) 474–7570. Seventy-nine units with cable television, pool, sauna, and hot tub fill the inn. Laundry and restaurants nearby. $$–$$$

Santa Fe Accomodations. (800) 776–7669.

For More Information

Chamber of Commerce. (505) 983–7317; www.santafechamber.com.

Visitors Bureau. 201 West Marcy Street; (800) 777–CITY; www.santafe.org.

Annual Community **Events**

SATURDAY OF THE FOURTH OF JULY WEEKEND
Pancake Breakfast. On the plaza; 7:00 A.M. to noon. This is a charitable event sponsored by the United Way. There is music, an antique car show, puppet shows, and games. Somehow the weather is always perfect, and everyone has a good meal and a good time. Go early.

JULY AND AUGUST
Spanish and Indian Markets. On the plaza; (505) 982–2226 (Spanish Market–late July) and (505) 983–5220 (Indian Market–late August). These two international art shows literally double Santa Fe's population for these weekends. There are artists from all over the United States, Mexico, and Canada for the Indian Market. The Spanish Market showcases both traditional and contemporary Southwestern art. If they interest you, they are not to be missed (make your hotel reservations early); if they don't, it's better to be out of town because you can't avoid them.

FRIDAY AFTER LABOR DAY
La Fiesta de Santa Fe. Plaza and Fort Marcy Park; (505) 988–7575. In 1712 this fiesta was established to honor the peaceful reoccupation of Santa Fe by Don Diego de Vargas in 1692. As such, it is the oldest community festival in the United States. The town picks a Queen (and her court) and a Don Diego (and his seventeen-man retinue). There are parades with these players, another one for dressed-up pets, arts and crafts, and a fabulous fireworks display at the burning of Zozobra (Old Man Gloom), a relatively recent addition to the fiesta.

DECEMBER
Christmas Eve on Canyon Road. A big, beautiful celebration. People stroll up the road, stopping at bonfires along the way to sing carols, sip cider, and roast marshmallows. There are *farolitos* ("little lanterns") everywhere to light your way. Most of the galleries are open, too, and offer **free** cookies and punch.

Northeast
New Mexico

N orelast New Mexico, where the fertile plains meet the Sangre de Cristo Mountains (the tail end of the Rockies), is the link to much of our Western history, from the Santa Fe Trail to the Atchison, Topeka & Santa Fe Railroad to Route 66. It is a wonderful, often overlooked, part of the state. There is no other place where it all came together so well, so go out and explore. Doc Holliday once owned a saloon in Las Vegas, and Billy the Kid relaxed in the hot springs of Montezuma. Near Raton, a quaint mining town a few miles from the Colorado border, there is Capulin Volcano, where you and your kids can hike into the 10,000-year-old cinder cone. Close by, the Whittington Center, the largest rifle range in the world, gives panoramic views of the wheel ruts of the great wagon trains that traveled along the Santa Fe Trail. From the famous town of Cimarron, where Jesse James, Annie Oakley, and Wyatt Earp stayed at the St. James Hotel, to the historic railroad terminal of the "original" Las Vegas, it is this part of New Mexico that defines "Western."

Raton

North on Interstate 25 at U.S. Highway 64. An information center is located at the intersection of Second Street and US 64/87.

In 1866 "Uncle Dick" Whootten blasted and graded a 27-mile road through the then-narrow Raton Pass on the Santa Fe Trail, charging every wagon, outlaw, and cowboy

NORTHEAST

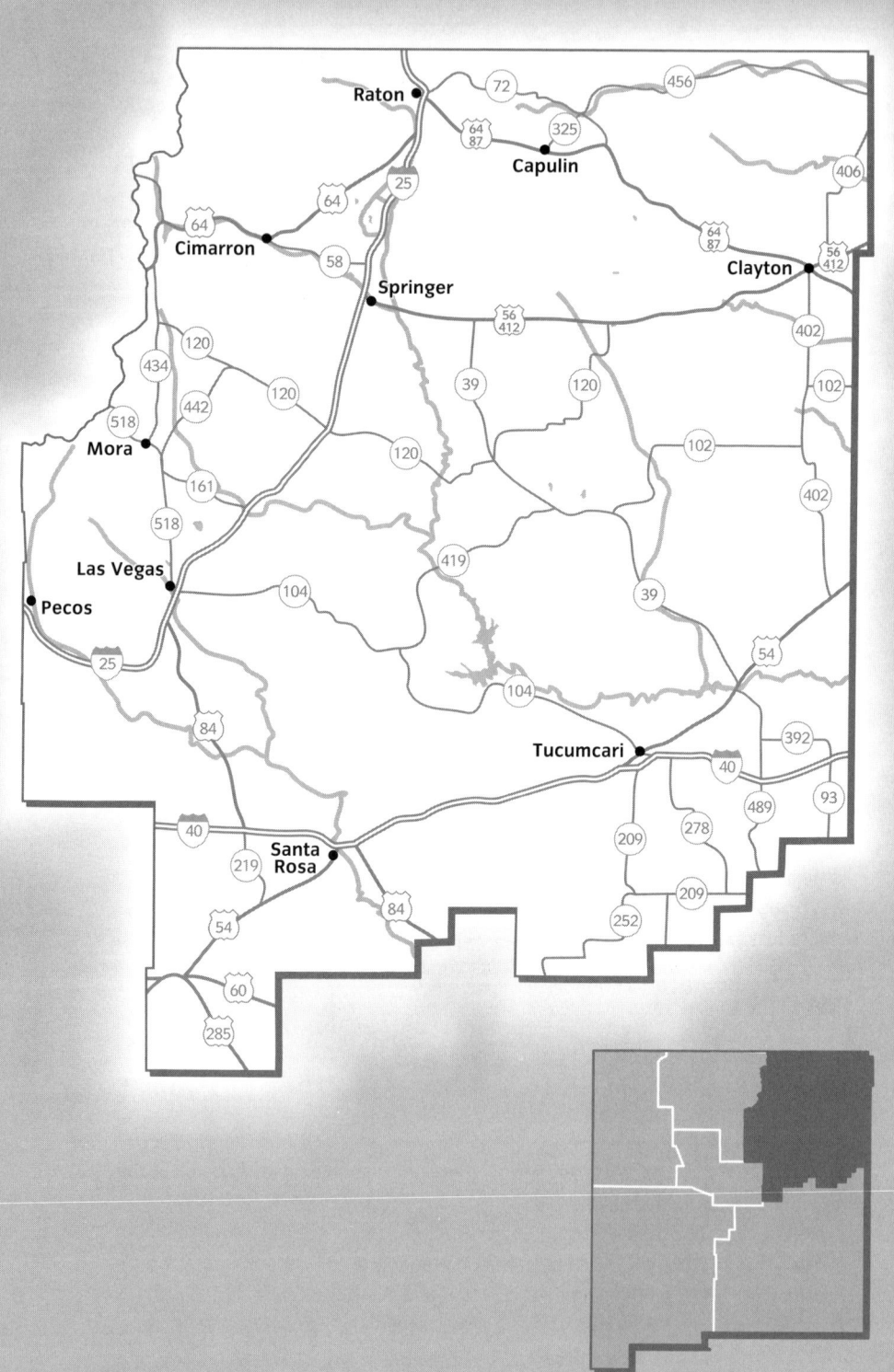

$1.50 to pass (letting the natives go through at no charge, however). The town of Raton (thought to be named for the kangaroo rat that is prevalent here) emerged in 1870 from the Willow Springs freight stop a little beyond the pass on the Santa Fe Trail. In 1879 trail travel changed to train travel both when the Atchison, Topeka & Santa Fe Railroad laid tracks crossing the Raton Pass (that was the end of Mr. Whootten's tollbooth, too) and when invaluable coal deposits attracted early settlers and Eastern businessmen to this town. With its railroad yards and nearby coalfields, Raton came to be known as the "Pittsburgh of the West." Coal mining is still the major source of income for the county. A walk through Raton's Historic District is a 5-block excursion that will take you around the town's original business district and back to the 1890s, when the city thrived.

Raton Museum (ages 10 to 12)
216 South First Street (in the old Coors Building); (505) 445–8979. Open from June through September, Tuesday through Saturday 9:00 a.m. to 5:00 P.M. Call for off-season schedule. Admission: Free.

Brings local history to life in the displays of the mining, ranching, and railroad equipment used by the Italian, Irish, and Slavic immigrant miners and in the collections of the records of some original settlers.

Shuler Theatre (ages 10 to 12)
131 North Second Street; (505) 445–4746. Hours: Monday through Friday 8:00 A.M. to 5:00 P.M.

Home to old Raton's opera, its firehouse, and city offices, this eighty-year-old rococo building is worth a visit if only to show your kids what it was like to go to the theater "once upon a time." Gold filigree decorates the exclusive box seats, the ceiling looks like a gilded sky, and the ornate woodwork drips from every corner. The town still uses the facility to stage local plays and touring shows.

Sugarite Canyon State Park (all ages)
9 miles northeast of Raton along Highways 72 and 526; (505) 445–5607. Admission: $5.00 for the day, $10.00 for overnight (RV hookups and sewer services, add $4.00 each).

This year-round park sits between two mesas along the banks of the Chicorico Creek. It has camping and picnicking areas, RV electric hookups, a visitor center, nature paths, and two pristine lakes, Alice and Maloya (stocked with trout), as well as shower facilities. There

Shuler **Theatre**

Check out the New Deal Art mural by Manville Chapman in the Shuler Theatre's foyer. There are more murals by Chapman and William Warder in El Portal Hotel on 101 North Third Street.

Other Things **to Do**

Maxwell National Wildlife Refuge (all ages). Take I–25 to exit 426, go
west to village of Maxwell (2 blocks), then north on Highway 445 for 3D 4
mile to Highway 505. Go 3 miles west until you see the entrance; (505) 375
2331. Open year-round (contact station is open from 7:30 A.M. to 4:00 P.M.).
Admission: **Free.** If your family enjoys bird-watching, be sure to visit the
refuge. During the fall and winter months, ducks and geese by the hundreds
make it a stopover. It's less exciting in the spring and summer months; still, it
has campsites and fishing facilities (no permit required) and is a good rest
spot in the warmer months. Restrooms are available at the contact station; pit
toilets are on the grounds.

are also the ruins of an abandoned coal miners' camp for the kids to run through. In winter, your family can enjoy the cross-country ski routes, ice-fishing, and sledding. If you
want to go camping, there are two campsites: Soda Pocket (open from Easter until Hal-
loween, weather permitting) and on Lake Alice (open year-round).

Annual **Community Events**

MID-JUNE
Santa Fe Trail Rendezvous. Cole Canyon, NRA Whittington Center;
cap-n-ball.com/raton

FOURTH OF JULY WEEKEND
Annual Balloon Fiesta. La Mesa Airfield;
(800) 638–6161

MID-AUGUST
Raton Arts and Crafts Fair. Ripley Park; (800)
638–6161

MID-SEPTEMBER
**Raton International Art
Show and Exhibit.** Ripley
Park; (800) 638–6161

Where to Eat

All-Seasons Family Restaurant. 1616 Cedar Street; (505) 445–9889. $–$$

La Cosina Cafe. 745 South Third Street; (505) 445–9675. New Mexico specialties as well as grilled cheese sandwiches and hamburgers. Open 11:00 A.M. to 2:00 P.M. and 5:00 to 8:00 P.M. Monday through Friday. $–$$

Pappas Sweet Shoppe. 1201 South Second Street; (505) 445–9811. Offers cloth-covered tables, a solid menu, and reasonable prices when the moment comes to dress up a little bit and enjoy a pleasant meal. Open 11:00 A.M. to 2:00 P.M. and 5:00 to 9:00 P.M. daily. $–$$$

Where to Stay

Hearts Desire Bed and Breakfast. 301 North Second Street; (505) 445–1000. A most engaging place, its late-Victorian charm gives your stay in one of four rooms an old-time quality. It's a roomy house that welcomes children. A cup of tea in the red-flocked living room is a special sensation for all the family to enjoy. $$–$$$

Holiday Classic. 473 Clayton Road (US 87); (505) 445–5555. Open twenty-four hours; there are eighty-six rooms. Heated indoor pool, laundry facilities, cable television, gift shop, game room with arcade. Restaurant and lounge on premises. $$

Oasis Motel. 1445 South Second Street; (505) 445–2766. Open twenty-four hours. Family owned and operated since 1954, the Oasis has fourteen spacious rooms and an adjoining restaurant. $–$$

Raton KOA campground. 1330 South Second Street; (505) 445–3488. Playground, arcade. Its fifty-four sites includes two cabins. $

For More Information

Chamber of Commerce. (505) 445–3689 or (800) 638–6161; www.raton.info.

Cimarron

US 64 at Highway 58 and Highway 21.

What fan of cowboy movies hasn't heard of Cimarron? Located on the Mountain Branch of the Santa Fe Trail, this truly Wild West town was settled around a stagecoach station in 1841, which served as a central meeting place for the area. In 1865 it became the property of Lucien B. Maxwell (buffalo hunter, entrepreneur, and Kit Carson's best buddy) after he had married into the family of one of the owners and had bought out the other. The Maxwell Land Grant, which extended over gold deposits, timber country, and grasslands, covered 1.74 million acres or three times the size of Rhode Island. Cimarron (meaning "wild or untamed place") was named for the area's untamed horses and sheep, but the name could easily apply to the people, attracting as it did the famous and infamous characters that enlivened that time. As both a destination and a passageway, it was a critical location for the settling (or taming) of the West and came to be known as the "Cowboy Capital of Northern New Mexico."

St. James Hotel (all ages) 🍴 ⊝ 🏛
Highways 21 and 64; (505) 376–2664 or (866) 472–5019. Room rate: $60 to $120.

Cimarron's biggest attraction was built in 1872 by Henri Lambert, who was supposedly the chef for Presidents Abraham Lincoln and Ulysses S. Grant. The hotel's present dining room was originally a Wild West saloon and the stage for murder, mayhem, and the likes of Annie Oakley, Frederic Remington, and Billy the Kid. Here Buffalo Bill Cody organized his Wild West shows and hosted lavish Christmas parties for the kids of Cimarron. Lew Wallace, an early New Mexican governor, wrote some of *Ben Hur* here and Zane Grey, *Fighting Caravans*. Have the kids try to count the twenty-nine bullet holes in the ceiling. While you and the kids are enjoying a civilized meal, you can imagine a time when you kept your back to the wall and one hand on your holster. The hotel is thought to be haunted by at least three spirits, two of which have rooms kept for them. You can have these rooms pointed out to you as well as those in which Wyatt Earp, Jesse James, and Annie Oakley slept. The hotel was remodeled in 1985. There are thirteen rooms beautifully decorated in the Victorian style. Each is unique and is named for a famous boarder. So authentic are they, that there are no phones or televisions, although there is an annex to the hotel with ten rooms that offer these amenities (OK, perhaps not with the same flair). Be sure to make reservations, especially if you plan to stay on a Wednesday or Tuesday night during the summer (these are the nights that the Philmont Ranch changes occupancy and the hotel is likely to be packed with Boy Scouts). Besides the elegant dining room and a diner-style restaurant (serving three inexpensive meals a day), there's a good coffee shop in the back if the kids need a break, as well as a well-stocked gift shop for both grown-ups and children to find a souvenir.

Annual **Community Events**

FOURTH OF JULY
Maverick Club Rodeo and Parade. Rodeo Grounds; (505) 376–2417.

LABOR DAY WEEKEND
Old Cimarron Days. Downtown; (505) 376–2417. Fine arts and crafts festival, with duck races!

Old Aztec Mill (ages 10 to 12)

Highway 21, 1 block south of the St. James Hotel. (505) 376–2913. Open May through September, Monday through Saturday 9:00 A.M. to 5:00 P.M., Sunday 1:00 to 5:00 P.M., closed Thursday. Admission: $2.00 for adults, $1.00 for children under 12 and senior citizens.

Right across from the hotel and inside the gristmill that furnished grain to Fort Union and the Ute Indians when Cimarron was the agency headquarters is the museum, which houses both a mix of regional artifacts of an earlier time and Boy Scout memorabilia.

Philmont Scout Ranch (all ages)

Highway 21, 5 miles south of Cimarron; (505) 376–2281. Philmont Museum open daily June through August, 8:00 A.M. to 6:00 P.M. (closed Sunday September through May). Kit Carson Museum open daily June 1 through August 22, 8:00 A.M. to 5:00 P.M. Admission to the museums: Free.

Oklahoma oilman Waite Phillips gave this property to the Boy Scouts of America in the late 1930s. Philmont, the first National Boy Scout Camp ever established, now hosts thousands of young men from all over the world who come each summer to learn wilderness survival skills. Whether or not you have Scouts in the family, you'll find this an amazing place. Buffalo and deer graze throughout the 137,000-acre ranch. There's also a gorgeous Mediterranean-style mansion, the Villa Philamonte, that you can tour (don't miss the Trophy Room with its mounted buffalo heads). The **Philmont Museum** has a collection of cowboy and Indian memorabilia that includes the library of Edward Thompson Seton, the naturalist and founder of the Boy Scouts of America. What's fun, too, is the **Kit Carson Museum.** It's farther out on the property, off Highway 21 by another 5 miles or so, in a place called Rayado. You don't necessarily learn a lot more about Colonel Carson, but it is an interesting interpretive museum run by Philmont volunteers. They live on site and are dressed in period costume. You are guided in and around a nineteenth-century village into a central square, where you are left to explore on your own. If you go there around lunchtime, you can sample the food being prepared over cookfires and in the *hornos* (small, outdoor beehive-shaped ovens), where volunteer guides bake bread.

Colin Neblett Wildlife Area and Cimarron Canyon State Park (all ages)

Between Eagle Nest and Cimarron on US 64; (505) 377–6271.

At more than 33,000 acres, Colin Neblett Wildlife Area is New Mexico's largest state-run wildlife park, which is home to large populations of elk, deer, bear, raptors, and songbirds.

• **Cimarron Canyon State Park.** 8 miles east of Eagle Nest along Route 64; (505) 377–6271. Admission: $5.00

per vehicle for the day ($10.00 for overnight), $4.00 electric hookup. There are camping facilities where you and the kids can fish for brown trout and climb up to the Cimarron Palisades (massive 400-foot-high granite outcroppings).

Elliott S. Barker Wildlife Area (all ages)
15 miles northwest of Cimarron; (505) 445–2311.

The refuge offers 5,400 acres of wildlife habitat. Hunting in season.

Where to Eat

Cree-Mee Drive In. 31083 U.S. Highway 64; (505) 376–2480. Family-owned. Open daily 9:00 A.M. to 9:00 P.M. $

Heck's Hungry Traveler. Highway 64; (505) 376–2574. Try their huge Heck-of-a-Burger or their Cimarron Roll. Open daily 6:15 A.M. to 8:00 P.M. $–$$

Simple Simon's Pizza. 253 East Ninth Street; (505) 376–2130. Good local pizza place. Try a slice with green chile! Open daily 11:00 A.M. to 8:00 P.M. $–$$

Where to Stay

Casa del Gavilan Bed and Breakfast. Highway 21 south of US 64; (505) 376–2246. $$–$$$

Cimarron Inn and RV Park. 212 East Tenth Street; (505) 376–2268 or (800) 546–2244. Twelve comfortable rooms and twelve RV sites with full hookups (including showers) are available. Weekly and monthly rates available. Laundry and shopping 1 block away. Pets welcome. $

Johnson's Cabins on the River. 161 West Thirteenth Street; (505) 376–2210. Three private cabins are located in a secluded area next to the Cimarron River. Each cabin includes kitchenette and a full bathroom.

Designed for smaller families (each includes one big bed and cots). Fishing access is sometimes available. No phone or television. Pets welcome. $–$$

Kit Carson Inn. Highway 64 East; (505) 376–2288. Thirty-nine simple and quiet rooms with cable television fill the inn. Restaurant on premises. $$

For More Information

Chamber of Commerce. (505) 376–2417; www.cimarronnm.com.

Visitor Center. 104 North Lincoln Avenue; (505) 376–2417.

Springer

I–25 at U.S. Highway 56.

Springer began as a railroad worker camp near the Cimarron cutoff of the Santa Fe Trail in 1879. It then developed from traffic flowing in the other direction, as it became a shipping point for cattle going east to Chicago and Kansas City. It was named for two prominent brothers who had some influence in the area.

Dorsey Mansion (all ages)

In nearby Chico Spring on US 56, 30 miles northeast of Springer; (505) 375–2222. Tours are by appointment only. Admission: $3.00 for adults, $1.00 for kids under 6.

Getting to this unique house is half the fun as your car bounces along a typically New Mexican dirt road. In 1878 Senator Stephen Dorsey, a carpetbagger and sometime reprobate, started building his dream house in the middle of the empty plain that he owned. By 1886 when the house was completed, it had a log cabin wing with a crenellated stone tower attached to it and a stone castle addition decorated with gargoyles and the faces of Dorsey's relatives carved into the ornate stonework. This bizarre thirty-six-room structure features a billiards room, a grandiose but now empty lily pond with three islands, and an art gallery. Between 1892, when Dorsey left the area (some say to avoid angry creditors), and the early 1970s, the mansion was in turn a tuberculosis sanitarium, a post office, a private residence, and a general store before it achieved museum status.

Santa Fe Trail Museum (ages 10 to 12)

606 Maxwell Avenue; (505) 483–5554. Open Memorial Day through Labor Day, 10:00 A.M. to 4:00 P.M. Tuesday through Saturday and from 1:00 to 4:00 P.M. Sunday; closed the rest of the year Monday through Friday. Admission: $2.00 for adults, $1.50 for kids 10–17, kids 9 and under free.

Trail-history exhibits and pioneer artifacts are located in this restored, 1881 former county courthouse.

Annual Community Events

AUGUST

Colfax County Fair. Fairgrounds; (505) 445–8071. Quilt contest, livestock shows, rodeo, and barbecue.

Where to Eat

Dairy Delite. 42 U.S. Highway 56; (505) 483–2813. Good, clean local spot for a burger and a milkshake. $

Rebecca's. 801 Railroad Avenue; (505) 483–2985. Mexican and American food. Open every day from 7:00 A.M. to 8:00 P.M. $–$$

Where to Stay

Brown Hotel and Cafe Bed and Breakfast. 302 Maxwell Avenue; (505) 483–2269. There are eleven lovely rooms (with shared bathrooms) decorated in the Victorian style.

Full breakfasts included. Cafe open Monday through Friday 6:00 A.M. to 8:00 P.M., Saturday to 2:00 P.M., and Sunday 7:00 A.M. to 2:00 P.M. Laundry and shopping across the street. $–$$

The Oasis Motel. 1001 Railroad Avenue; (505) 483–2777. Seventeen quiet comfortable rooms with cable television fill the motel. Shopping, restaurants, and laundry facilities nearby. $–$$

For More Information

Chamber of Commerce. (505) 483–2998.

Mora

Highway 518 at Highway 434.

Settled by farmers in 1818, the village of Mora was originally called L'eau des Morts (Water of the Dead) because a French beaver-trapping party found human bones in what is now called the Mora River. Mora County is one of the more remote areas of northern New Mexico. Great expanses of land hide hamlets made up of nothing more than a few adobe casitas and a chapel. Early residents were an eclectic mix of Spanish, Mexican, Irish, German, Syrian, and French ancestry.

Fort Union National Monument (all ages)
23 miles northeast of Las Vegas off I–25 and Highway 161; (505) 425–8025; www.nps.gov/foun. Admission: $3.00 per person. Open from Memorial Day to Labor Day, 8:00 A.M. to 6:00 P.M.; 8:00 A.M. to 4:00 P.M. the rest of the year. Closed Christmas, Thanksgiving, and New Year's Day.

This famous fort, the largest military encampment in the Southwest, guarded the Santa Fe Trail. The monument shows the ruins of the third structure known as Fort Union. It was from this garrison that Gen. H. H. Sibley resigned his post to fight for the Confederate army and from here that Union soldiers, volunteers who had come from Colorado, marched out to squelch his army and the Confederate hopes of securing the West (and the gold and silver mines therein) for themselves in the battle at Glorieta Pass. Your kids will like the walking tours of the monument because there are interpretive audio stations along the trail and even bugle calls wafting across the grounds. If you search, you'll find ruts from the wagon trains that you can follow, too. The park provides areas for picnics but no camping.

Salman Raspberry Ranch and Cafe and La Cueva Mill (all ages)

Junction of Highways 518 and 442; (505) 387–2900. Ranch and gift shop open daily in the summer, 9:00 A.M. to 5:00 P.M.; in the winter, Thursday through Monday 9:00 A.M. to 4:00 P.M. Cafe serves food during raspberry season, generally August through September.

The ranch is a working farm and a gigantic raspberry patch. Salman's also maintains wild-flower gardens near La Cueva Mill and the store. In the summer, the owners open the antique post office and store of the old village of La Cueva. They sell some of their freshly grown asparagus and corn, as well as their own famous raspberry jam and vinegar and dried flowers. If you visit between the end of August and mid-October, you can also pick your own raspberries. Although the mill no longer functions (sorry, you can't go in), it is a beautiful adobe structure, which owner David Salman has restored, and is worth a few photos. Enjoy lunch at the Salman Ranch Cafe. Raspberry ice-cream sundaes are a specialty there.

Cleveland Roller Mill Historical Museum (all ages)

2 miles northwest of the village of Mora on Highway 518; (505) 387–2645. Open Saturday and Sunday from Memorial Day until Labor Day, 10:00 A.M. to 4:00 P.M. Admission: $2.00 for adults, $1.00 for kids age 16 and under.

This is another attraction in this beautiful valley, once considered the breadbasket of New Mexico. One of the several mills that operated near Mora at the turn of the twentieth century, it continued to serve the residents of the area until 1957. It is one of the few intact and operating mills in the Southwest. In the nineteenth century it ground thousands of pounds of coarse wheat for the U.S. Army at Fort Union. The parking lot is huge and can accommodate RVs (no overnights, though). There's a picnic area to fit most small family reunions.

Check Out . . .

- **Junior Ranger Program** at Fort Union (ages 6 to 15). This national park program is a scavenger hunt/trivia game designed for kids passing through the park. Have them pick up a booklet and turn it in completed to get a patch of certification. More important than the patch, of course, is the chance for kids to better interact with the park by learning interesting facts and strengthening their wilderness skills.

Annual **Cleveland Millfest**

Every Labor Day weekend, at the Cleveland Roller Hill Museum, the Friends of the Mill hold a festival featuring traditional music, food, arts, and crafts.

Morphy Lake State Park (all ages)
7 miles south of Mora on Highway 94; (505) 387–2328. Admission: $5.00 for the day, $8.00 for overnight.

This pack-in, pack-out park offers camping, fishing, boating, picnicking, and hiking. Bring your own drinking water; the park has none. Open in spring and summer only.

Coyote Creek State Park (all ages)
17 miles north of Mora along Highway 434; (505) 387–2328. Admission: $5.00 for the day, $10.00 for overnight.

This park has private campgrounds shaded by cottonwoods, ponderosa pines, and willow trees. There are facilities for picnicking, fishing, and hiking, as well as showers.

Check **Out** . . .

- **Wagon Mound and Bean Day Festival.** Heading north on I–25 a group of volcanic mesas jut skyward just over a rise on the road. One of them, which resembles a covered wagon, was the last important landmark for those on the Santa Fe Trail. The village of Wagon Mound holds an annual Bean Day Festival on Labor Day weekend with a rodeo, barbecue, and dancing. Call (505) 666–2697 for more specifics.
- **Victory Ranch.** Highway 434 (1 mile north of Mora); (505) 387–2254; www.victoryranch.com. Admission: **Free** (if you want to feed the alpacas, it's $2.00 for adults, $1.00 for children 12 and under). Feed the woolly alpacas. These animals are close relatives of the llama and are more distantly related to the camel. Spinning and weaving demonstrations, too. Open daily 10:00 A.M. to 4:00 P.M.

Where to Eat

Hatcha's Cafe. Highway 518; (505) 387–9299. It feels like you're in your mama's kitchen here (and she's cooking for you, too). Try their Navajo tacos (sopaipillas filled with beans and beef) and their great Sunday brunch. Open Monday through Friday 10:00 A.M. to 8:00 P.M. and Sunday 8:00 A.M. to 3:00 P.M. The restaurant is closed Saturday. $–$$

Where to Stay

Mora Inn. 2 miles northeast of Mora in Cleveland on Highway 518 (across from the Cleveland Roller Mill Historical Museum);

(505) 387–5230. The motel has nine quiet, comfortable rooms with television and full bath. Restaurant on premises. $–$$

Totem Guest Ranch. Rociada (take Highway 94 south out of Mora, then west on Highway 105 for 3 miles); (505) 425–8929. There are three full-service units with kitchenettes and full baths. Horseback riding and mountain bikes for guests' use. Laundry and shopping nearby. $$–$$$

For More Information

Mora Chamber of Commerce and Tourism Office. (505) 387–6072; www.moravalley.com.

Las Vegas

Off I–25, exits 343, 345, and 347. Welcome Center at the junction of Grand Avenue (Highway 65) and New Mexico Avenue.

Home to the Paleo Indians in 8000 B.C., Las Vegas's (The Meadows) history dates to 1821, when Luis Maria C. de Baca petitioned the Mexican government for a parcel of land. Citizens of Spain (and then Mexico) were allowed to keep the land if they farmed it for four years. It was ideally situated for sheep raising, but the residents of the time, the Comanches, liked it too, and no one had petitioned *them*. Mr. C. de Baca was granted his parcel in 1825, but the Comanches kept him from occupying all but a small portion of it. The next chapter begins in 1835, when a group of Spanish settlers were granted another parcel. This time it came with the condition that a plaza be built not only as a meeting place for the settlers and their families, but also as a central area of defense against the still-raiding Comanches. Travel on the Santa Fe Trail was increasing, too, and the plaza quickly became a place to trade. On August 15, 1846, Gen. Stephen Watts Kearny arrived and claimed the land for the United States. He made Las Vegas a military headquarters until Fort Union was built five years later. Las Vegas was the territo-

Self-Guided **Walking and Driving Tour**

This tour includes the more than 900 historic sites and buildings that put Las Vegas on the map. Tour booklets are available at the visitor center at 727 North Grand Avenue (505–425–8803).

rial capital of the Union during the Confederate occupation of Santa Fe in 1862, and the city remained largely Spanish until the Atchison, Topeka & Santa Fe Railroad arrived in 1879. Soon it was the most important commercial and social gathering place in the region.

The city is a great deal quieter nowadays, a shadow of its former self, but there are still many interesting sights for you and the kids to enjoy (there are more than 900 buildings listed on the National Register of Historic Places). There are three different self-guided walking tours (check with the Welcome Center), which might be the place to start if the weather is good.

Bridge Street and the Plaza (all ages)

Old Town Plaza is the center of the historic district and another area where children can imagine life when cowboys roamed the streets and Doc Holliday (who owned a saloon and a dental office near the railroad) pulled teeth. For the most part, Las Vegas is best seen on foot or from a stroller (see sidebar on walking tours in Las Vegas). Local business people are working to revitalize this Wild West town, so there are plenty of charming, interesting shops and coffeehouses to visit along Bridge Street, the main business street right off the historic plaza. One of the more interesting places isn't really a tourist sight at all, but an old-fashioned drug store. If you pop into **Plaza Drug** on the corner of Old Town Plaza and Bridge Street, you'll enter one of those amazing time warps found only in small Western towns. Here's where you can show your kids what a pharmacy looked like fifty years ago. Then you can all hitch up to the soda fountain for a Coke with a dash of cherry. **El Tecolote** (the owl) is along Bridge Street, too. It has old Western saddles and other Wild West paraphernalia. Your family will love poking through boxes of old spurs or figuring out what the branding iron symbols mean. **The Plaza Hotel** (northwest corner of the plaza) was restored during its centennial. It is a faithful re-creation of the classic hotel of the 1880s West and is listed on the National Register of Historic Places.

City Museum and Rough Riders Memorial Collection (ages 10 to 12)

727 Grand Avenue; (505) 454–1401. Open Monday through Friday 9:00 A.M. to 4:00 P.M. year-round, plus Saturday 10:00 A.M. to 3:00 P.M. from May through October. Free.

The City Museum provides a glimpse of 1880s frontier life through a collection of household items, clothing, arms, and ranching and farming gear. The first Rough Riders reunion, led by Teddy Roosevelt, was held here in 1899 after the cowboy volunteers helped Cuba gain its independence from Spain, and the museum contains some pertinent memorabilia.

Carnegie Library (all ages)
500 National Avenue; (505) 454–1401.

Built in 1903, this library, one of the originals in the Carnegie Library system, was modeled architecturally after Thomas Jefferson's home, Monticello. It still operates as a library and might offer a good storytime break.

Montezuma Castle and Hot Springs (all ages)
West of Las Vegas on Highway 65. The school offers tours of the castle on occasional Saturdays; call (505) 454–4221 to make a reservation. Hot springs are free.

A former Santa Fe Railroad resort built in 1882, the Montezuma Castle and Hot Springs was meant to lure tourists from all over the world, but it kept burning down. For a decade, at least (in between fires), it served customers such as Rutherford B. Hayes, Ulysses S. Grant, Kaiser Wilhelm, and Emperor Hirohito. It is even said that Billy the Kid went to these springs to have a soak when he was visiting Doc Holliday. Dubbed the "Phoenix," it was in the end a financial embarrassment, and in 1903 the railroad finally gave up its ambition and its interest in the property. The land and castle is now the property of the **Armand Hammer United World College,** a small gathering place for students from around the world to learn about world peace and multicultural harmony. The college recently repaired and renovated the castle to be used as dormitories.

Check Out . . .

- **Sapello and the Star Hill Inn.** (505) 425–5605; www.starhillinn.com. Thirteen miles north of Las Vegas is the town of Sapello and the Star Hill Inn. The inn is a bit pricey, but this could be a memorable visit for everyone in the family because Star Hill has an astronomy center. There are three powerful telescopes on the observation deck off the library, and a 6,000 mm scope housed nearby. The owners host astronomy, birding, and art seminars throughout the year. Each of these special weekends studies a facet of the astronomical grid of the New Mexican skies.

- **Hermit's Peak.** I–25, west of Las Vegas. This 10,263-foot granite outcropping was an important landmark on the Santa Fe Trail. From 1863 to 1867 it was also home to Giovanni Marie Augustini, an Italian recluse and holy man who had walked the trail from Kansas. When he wasn't healing the sick or creating well-publicized miracles, the hermit was carving crucifixes and other religious articles that he traded for food. After spending four years here, Augustini moved to the Organ Mountains in southwestern New Mexico, where he was found murdered in 1869.

Storrie Lake State Park (all ages)

4 miles north of Las Vegas via Highway 518; (505) 425–7278. Admission: $5.00 per vehicle for the day, $8.00 and $10.00 (primitive and developed sites respectively) for overnight ($14.00 for hookup).

This is a good place to windsurf, fish, boat, water ski, camp, and picnic. There is an annual fishing derby on the Saturday before Easter; call (505) 425–8631 for more information.

McAllister Lake (all ages)

8 miles east of Las Vegas on Highway 104; (505) 445–2311.

The lake, part of the Las Vegas National Wildlife Refuge, offers recreation year-round. Eagles fly in during the wintertime, as do various waterfowl. You can also camp and fish for northern pike and trout.

Las Vegas National Wildlife Refuge (all ages)

5 miles southeast of Las Vegas on Routes 104 and 281; (505) 425–3581. Visitor center open Monday through Friday 8:00 A.M. to 4:30 P.M. Admission: **Free.**

The refuge includes the magical **Gallinas Canyon Nature Trail.** The rangers won't tell you about this one; you need to ask about it at the visitor center. It's well worth the trip.

Gallinas Canyon (all ages)

Take Hot Springs Boulevard (Highway 65) north and continue 6 miles past Montezuma Castle. For maps and information on hiking in the area, stop at the Visitor Center at 501 South Grand Avenue, or call (505) 454–4101.

Here you can find El Porvenir (The Future) Campground and numerous backcountry hiking trails into Carson National Forest. You can also hike up to Hermit's Peak (8 miles round-trip) for the spectacular views. There are two other well-marked trails off this one: Dispensas Trail (also 8 miles) and Porvenir Canyon Trail (28 miles). In the winter months, there are also cross-country trails and a skating area on the Gallinas River.

Where to Eat

Charlie's Rib Barbecue. 227 South Pacific Street; (505) 454–7246. Children's plates are available from $2.95 to $4.95. Open Tuesday through Saturday 11:00 A.M. to 8:00 P.M. $–$$$

El Rialto. 141 Bridge Street; (505) 454–0037. Excellent, well-priced Mexican food. Hours: Monday through Saturday 10:30 A.M. to 9:00 P.M. $–$$

Landmark Grill in the Plaza Hotel. 230 Plaza Street; (505) 425–3591. Restaurant serves breakfast, lunch, and dinner in addition to Sunday brunch. They also will pack lunches for family outings. Open 7:00 A.M. to 2:30 P.M. and 5:00 to 9:00 P.M. $$–$$$

Where to Stay

Carriage House B&B (ages 10 to 12). 925 Sixth Street; (505) 454–1784. Wonderful old Victorian house with big wraparound porch and five units (some with private baths). Wonderful owners, too. $$–$$$

Annual Community Events

SATURDAY BEFORE EASTER
Storrie Lake Fishing Derby. (505) 425–8631

MAY 5
Cinco de Mayo. (505) 425–8631

FOURTH OF JULY
July Fiesta. Plaza Park; (505) 425–8631

AUGUST
San Miguel County Fair. (505) 454–1497

LATE AUGUST
People's Fair and Places with a Past. Carnegie Park; (505) 425–8631

DECEMBER
Main Street Holiday Program. (505) 425–8631

El Camino. 1152 North Grand Avenue; (505) 425–5994. This is a twenty-four-room family-run establishment. Small pets welcome at extra charge (approximately $6.00). Restaurant on premises (open daily 6:30 A.M. to 9:00 P.M.). $–$$

Inn on the Santa Fe Trail. 1133 Grand Avenue; (505) 425–6791 or (888) 448–8438. Updated thirty-two-room hacienda-style motel near the historic district. Laundry facilities available, as well as refrigerators, microwaves, and VCRs in some rooms. Pool. Complimentary continental breakfast. Children under 12 **free**. $$

Plaza Hotel. 230 Plaza Street; (505) 425–3591 or (800) 328–1882; www.plaza hotel-nm.com. The historic 1882 hotel has thirty-six rooms renovated for the modern traveler. Each room is decorated to reflect a certain style or famous guest. **Free** breakfast; children under 12 stay for **free**. Restaurant and bar on premises. Check out the Web site for special Internet rates. $$–$$$

Vegas RV Park. 504 Harris Road; (505) 425–5640. There are thirty well-maintained sites with full hookups here. Showerhouse, too. Right in town near shopping, laundry, and restaurants. $–$$

For More Information

Chamber of Commerce. 727 North Grand Avenue; (505) 425–8631 or (800) 832– 5947; www.lasvegasnewmexico.com.

Visitor Center. 501 South Grand Avenue; (505) 454–4101.

Pecos

I–25 at Highway 63, 21 miles east of Santa Fe.

This small Hispanic village in the upper Pecos River Valley was founded around 1700 and called Levy until 1883.

Pecos National Historic Park (all ages)

Highway 63, 2 miles south of Pecos; (505) 757–6414; www.nps.gov/peco. Open from Memorial through Labor Day 8:00 A.M. to 6:00 P.M., 8:00 A.M. to 5:00 P.M. the rest of the year. Admission: $3.00 per person.

The area of Pecos was inhabited 12,000 years ago by mammoth, bison, and camel hunters. About 500 years ago, the area around Pecos was populated by pottery makers, hunters, and jewelers who traded extensively with the Plains Indians. When Spanish explorers arrived in the 1540s, Pecos was among the most highly organized pueblos that they encountered. Continued contact with the Europeans and periods of extended drought led to famine and disease and the eventual evacuation of the pueblo in 1838, when the survivors walked to join their cousins at the Jémez Pueblo, north of Albuquerque. Next to the ruins of Pecos Pueblo—which rose four to five stories in height and contained 600 rooms—are the remains of seventeenth- and eighteenth-century Spanish colonial missions (great for games of hide-and-seek). The park, which recently acquired 5,500 acres of the Glorieta Civil War Battlefield and Greer Garson's Forked Lightning Ranch, now encompasses hundreds of archaeological sites as well as two structures: Kozlowski's Ranch (one of the stations on the Santa Fe Trail) and the Tex Austin House. Included are a visitor center, a 1¼-mile ruins trail, and 2½ miles of the Pecos River. It is a very beautiful site and a perfect spot for children to explore. Try to be there around sunset.

Glorieta Pass (ages 10 to 12)
I–25, 14 miles east of Santa Fe.

The decisive Civil War battle in New Mexico was fought at the summit of Glorieta Pass on March 28, 1862. Union troops dashed Southern hopes for a takeover of New Mexico—and ultimately the West—when a party of Union volunteers from Colorado burned Confederate supply wagons in Glorieta's Apache Canyon. The pass also served as a gateway through the mountains for Francisco Vasquez de Coronado's 1541 exploration of the plains in preparation for the Spanish friars' conversion expeditions of the 1600s, for Apache and Comanche entry into Pueblo country, and for the Santa Fe Trail excursions of the 1820s to 1880s.

Where to Eat

Casa de Herrera. Highway 63; (505) 757–6740. Open Monday through Saturday 11:00 A.M. to 2:00 P.M. and 5:00 to 8:00 P.M., Sunday 9:00 A.M. to 1:00 P.M. $–$$

Kristina's Restaurant. Highway 50; (505) 757–2662. Open daily 7:00 A.M. to 8:00 P.M. $–$$

Renate's. Highway 50, (505) 757–2626. Homey German dishes and baked goods. The sauerbraten is especially good, as is the rum cake. Open for lunch 11:00 A.M. to 2:00 P.M. Saturday and Sunday and for dinner 5:00 to 9:00 P.M. Wednesday through Monday. $–$$

Where to Stay

Because there are few accommodations central to Pecos, most visitors to the Pecos area stay in Santa Fe.

Los Pinos Guest Ranch. 20 miles north of Pecos on Highway 63 (take the Pecos exit from I–25 and keep going); (505) 757–6213; www.lospinosranchcom. Well-appointed log cabins among the aspen, spruce, and fir. Prices include all meals. **Note:** Children over the age of 6 only. Fishing (with a New Mexico license), horseback riding, and hiking available. $$–$$$

For More Information

State Bureau of Tourism. (800) 545–2040; www.pecosnewmexico.com.

Pigeon **Ranch**

I–25, 14 miles east of Santa Fe. This stagecoach stop along the Santa Fe Trail became famous as part of the Glorieta Pass Civil War battlefield in 1862. It is the only roofed structure to have withstood the battle.

Santa Rosa

I–40 east to the Santa Rosa exit at U.S. Highway 54.

This is Guadalupe County, another of those huge New Mexican areas with little population but a lot of wonderful outdoor opportunities to savor. If you drive from Albuquerque, it is actually one of the drier, flatter stretches of New Mexico; you can't quite believe that you're heading to a place that calls itself the "City of Natural Lakes." Originally settled on the banks of the Pecos River in the 1860s by Spanish ranchers and farmers, Santa Rosa is named for Santa Rosa de Lima, a Catholic saint, and the chapel that was dedicated to her. Like other towns in New Mexico, it blossomed in the 1880s when the railroad arrived, then again from the 1920s to the 1970s, when Route 66 was completed but before I–40 took travelers away from the town. Now people come for the attractions that have lasted; the nearby lakes and the fishing, boating, and swimming they afford (as well as the scuba diving at Blue Hole). Santa Rosa is a true oasis.

Blue Hole (ages 10 to 12)

Less than a mile from downtown Santa Rosa. Take Fifth Street from Will Rogers Drive, then go east (left) on Lake Drive, taking a right on Blue Hole Road shortly thereafter; (505) 472–3370. Admission: Free to swim, $8.00 to dive.

This is one of the more unusual spots in Santa Rosa. Set 5,000 feet above sea level, this is a bona fide natural scuba diving pool *cum* campsite. Only 80 feet in diameter, experts have gone down to 160 feet to an area called "the second chamber." The water is as clear as, well, water, and the temperature is a constant 64° F. An underground river fills the pool at 3,000 gallons per minute, so the water is replaced every six hours. Once underwater, you feel as if you're in an aquarium, not only because of the clarity of the water but also because of the various snails, plant life, fish, and sandy deposits. A nearby shop rents diving equipment, but in order to dive, you must obtain a permit from the Santa Rosa Police Department (on Fifth Street, just south of the Chamber of Commerce) and prove that you are a certified diver. Without this, you can only dive accompanied by a certified and insured instructor. Campsites are available.

Annual **Community Events**

MEMORIAL DAY
Santa Rosa Days. Park Lake (see Blue Hole entry above); (505) 472–3763.
Parade, raft race, fun run, fishing contest, etc.

AUGUST
Santa Rosa de Lima Fiesta. Santa Rosa de Lima Church; (505) 472–3724.
Entertainment, food, crafts, dancing, a mass, and the crowning of the Fiesta
Queen.

SEPTEMBER
Fun Run Santa Rosa Custom Car Show. Downtown; (505) 472–3763 or
(505) 472–1966.

Route 66 Festival and Pecos River Motorcycle Rally. (505) 472–3763.
Features Billy the Kid gunfight reenactment, motorcycles, entertainment, and
outdoor movies.

Santa Rosa Lake State Park (all ages)
7 miles north of Santa Rosa along Highway 91; (505) 472–3110. Admission: $5.00 per vehi-
cle, $10.00 per campsite ($14.00 with hookups).

The largest lake in the area, the surrounding park has all of the usual amenities of the New
Mexico State Park system as well as good fishing for catfish, bass, crappie, and walleye.
This lake is considered by many anglers to be one of the best fishing areas in the state,
even if it was built for water storage and flood control. A small visitor center is found
across the dam near the Corps of Engineers office, and camping is available in the two
campgrounds provided. Rocky Point has more than forty sites with hookups, water (restrooms have flush toilets and showers), and shelters (nice if you are in need of some
shade). Juniper Park is a less developed camping area, but it, too, has boat ramps, picnic
tables, and indoor plumbing. Among the many nature trails, one is especially designed for
wheelchairs (should work for strollers, too).

Other Things **to Do**

If the family's not all tuckered out from diving, or if everyone just has a han-
kering for a little baseball, on the way back to town there is a city-maintained
park around the corner on Lake Park Drive. There isn't any camping, but you
can swim, play tennis, or take a hot shower.

Where to Eat

Joseph's. 865 Will Rogers Drive; (505) 472–3361. Mexican food is the main fare at this eatery jammed with Route 66 memorabilia, but there are many typical American dishes, too. Moderately priced and a favorite of the locals. Open at 6:00 A.M. $$

Lake City Diner. 101 Fourth Street; (505) 472–5253. From pasta to enchiladas. Open Monday through Friday 4:00 to 10:00 P.M., Saturday 5:00 to 10:00 P.M. $–$$

Mateo's Family Restaurant. 500 Coronado Avenue; (505) 472–5720. Open daily from 7:00 A.M. to 7:30 P.M. $–$$

Where to Stay

Best Western Santa Rosa Inn. 3022 Will Rogers Drive; (505) 472–5877. Forty-four well-maintained rooms all with cable television, some with refrigerators. Outdoor pool. Small pets welcome. Restaurants and laundry facilities nearby. $$

Days Inn. 1830 Will Rogers Drive; (505) 472–5985. The inn offers forty-nine well-kept rooms with shopping and laundry nearby. Extra charge for pets ($3.00–$5.00). $$

Holiday Inn Express. 3300 Will Rogers Drive; (505) 472–5411. There are fifty rooms decorated in the southwestern style. Whirlpool and laundry facilities available. Small pets OK, too. Restaurants nearby. $$

For More Information

Visitor Center. Located in City Hall; 141 South Fifth Street; (505) 472–3763; www.santarosanm.org.

Tucumcari

I–40 at Highway 209 and Highway 104.

In 1926 the nation's first paved road linking the East and West Coasts entered New Mexico east of Tucumcari. When Route 66 captured the public's imagination as the road to endless fun and became one of the most traveled routes in America, Tucumcari was one of the main watering holes for those happy travelers. The town marked the halfway point between Amarillo, Texas, and Albuquerque, and as such, it flowered into a thriving tourist town, offering more than 2,000 hotel and motel rooms to indulge its visitors (they aren't going to let you forget this fact, so I can't either). The area's role as host to nomads began more than 10,000 years ago, when Folsom Man followed the path of the mastodons. Much later, the Apaches and Comanches made new tracks for the Goodnight and Loving cattle drives to follow. The dust around Tucumcari didn't settle until 1901, when the Rock Island Railroad isolated it as a construction site. The town is named for Tucumcari Mountain rising 1,000 feet above the surrounding plain, which had been used for many years not only as a landmark for travelers, but as a lookout point for the Comanches. There's some controversy about the origin of the name, which means "to lie in wait for someone

For Further **Reference**

Cuentos: Tales from the Hispanic Southwest by José Griego y Maestas and Rudolfo A. Anaya (Museum of New Mexico Press). Good bilingual storytelling.

or something to approach." Some defer to an old Apache love story involving two rivals for the chief's daughter, but this *is* Comanche territory, after all.

Tucumcari Historical Museum (all ages)

416 South Adams Street; (505) 461–4201; www.cityoftucumcari.com/museum. Open Monday through Saturday 8:00 A.M. to 6:00 P.M. Admission: $2.00 for adults, 50 cents for children.

Located in a two-story former schoolhouse, the museum houses such things as a pre-1900 windmill (how did they get it in there?), Folsom spearpoints (see Folsom Man in the Clayton listing), mammoth teeth and petrified wood, a 1926 firetruck, and an old-time nickelodeon. Most of the contents were donated by residents, so there is quite a mix here. Expect the unexpected. The museum also has several "reenactment" exhibits to illustrate the early history of Tucumcari. You'll find a typical cowboy's room and an early post office.

Conchas Lake State Park (all ages)

34 miles northwest of Tucumcari on Highway 104; (505) 868–2270. Admission: $5.00 for the day, $8.00 for primitive overnight camping, $10.00 for developed campsite ($4.00 extra with hookup).

One of the two man-made lakes saddling the city, it offers sailing, boating, and windsurfing access, as well as some great fishing at its three recreation sites. The central area is for picnicking and camping (with pit toilets). The north and south areas both feature boat launching ramps, marinas (you can rent boats if you didn't bring your own this time), restrooms, and grocery stores.

Ute Lake State Park (all ages)

30 miles northeast of Tucumcari along US 54 and Highway 540; (505) 487–2284. Admission: $5.00 for the day, $10.00 for overnight ($4.00 extra with hookup).

The fourth-largest park in New Mexico, and the other man-made lake near Tucumcari, is also another favorite spot for boating and fishing. There are two areas for RVs, boat ramps (and boats to rent), swimming holes, good fishing, and some primitive campsites on three separate campgrounds. Only the north area has plumbing to support showers and flushing toilets, but the main office has these if you're staying elsewhere in the park.

Annual Community Events

FOURTH OF JULY
July Fourth Celebration. Lake Logan, Ute Park; (505) 487–2284. Barbecue, fireworks, etc.

JULY
Route 66 Festival. (505) 461–1694. A three-day gathering featuring parades, chile cook-offs, antique car shows, music, and arts and crafts.

AUGUST
Quay County Fair. (505) 461–1694. Livestock exhibits, rides, food, and arts and crafts.

Where to Eat

Del's. 1202 East Tucumcari Boulevard; (505) 461–1740. Since the 1950s, Del's has been serving good New Mexican and American food at this classic Route 66 diner. Children's menu available. Truck and RV parking available, too. Open Monday through Saturday 7:00 A.M. to 9:00 P.M. $–$$

La Cita. 812 South First Street; (505) 461–0949. Mexican food, as well as steak and sandwiches. Open Monday through Saturday 10:30 A.M. to 9:00 P.M., Sunday to 2:00 P.M. $–$$

Lena's Home-Cooking. 112 East Main Street; (505) 461–1610. A good selection of homemade food. Open Monday through Friday 7:00 A.M. to 7:00 P.M., Saturday to 1:30 P.M. $–$$

Pow Wow Restaurant and Cantina. 801 West Tucumcari Boulevard; (505) 461–2587 or (800) 52POW–WOW. Broad selection of New Mexican, Italian, and American surf and turf. Children's menu. The kitchen is open daily 6:00 A.M. to 10:00 P.M. There's a live band Friday and Saturday to 1:00 A.M. $–$$$

Where to Stay

KOA Tucumcari. Route 54N Bypass; (505) 461–1841 or (800) KOA–1871; www. koakampgrounds.com. On historic Route 66, this campground with ninety sites offers views of the mesas. Playground, gift shop, and full hookups. $

Microtel Inn. 2420 South First Street; (505) 461–0600 or (888) 771–7171. The inn has fifty-three well-maintained rooms with an

Yucca

New Mexico's state flower is the yucca. Called "Our Lord's Candle" by early settlers, it is a narrow, conical-shaped wand with ivory blossoms (in the summertime) supported by broad, sawlike leaves at the base—hard to miss, and very beautiful.

indoor pool and cable television. Complimentary continental breakfast included. $–$$

Pow Wow Inn Best Western. 801 West Tucumcari Boulevard; (505) 461–0500 or (800) 52POW–WOW. Sixty-four southwestern-style rooms and suites fill the inn. Pool, playground, cable television, newly renovated lounge, gift shop, and restaurant on premises

(see Pow Wow Restaurant and Cantina). Pets welcome ($10 charge). $–$$

For More Information

Chamber of Commerce. (505) 461–1694 or (888) 664–7255; www. tucumcarinm.com.

Fort Bascom and **Comanche Raids**

Located 8 miles north of Tucumcari. The fort was erected in 1863 as a defense against the Comanches, who had effectively driven out the Jicarilla Apaches and by the 1860s had launched an unyielding campaign against Spanish and Anglo attempts to settle in the area. The fort was abandoned in 1870, although the Comanches weren't subdued until four years later.

Clayton

US 64/87 at US 56.

Did the caravans of homesteaders traveling the Cimarron cutoff of the Santa Fe Trail know that they were in the heart of dinosaur country? You can see the footprints of one and the wagon wheel tracks of another in abundance in Clayton. Clayton was founded in 1887 by the Colorado and Southern Railroad. Named for the son of ex-senator Stephen W. Dorsey (see Springer), one of the town's developers, Clayton, with its rich grasslands, became a major turn-of-the-century livestock shipping center.

Capulin Volcano National Monument (all ages)
30 miles east along US 64/87, then north on Highway 325; (505) 278–2201; www.nps.gov/cavo. Open daily 8:00 A.M. to 4:00 P.M. in winter, longer from Memorial Day to Labor Day. Admission: $3.00 per person, $5.00 per vehicle.

Although Capulin Volcano hasn't erupted in more than 10,000 years, this unusually symmetrical cinder cone volcano, which rises 1,200 feet above the surrounding plains, is considered merely dormant. Its name is Spanish for "chokecherry," which grows abundantly in the area. There are numerous trails to hike, including one that spirals up and around to the top of the volcano and others that circle the rim and lead into the crater. As you walk along, you get stunning vistas of four states: New Mexico, Colorado, Oklahoma, and Texas. A visitor center offers a library and natural history collection. During the summer, 15-minute ranger programs are offered several times a day.

Herzstein Memorial Museum (ages 10 to 12)
South Second and Walnut Streets; (505) 374–2977; www.herzsteinmuseum.org. Open Tuesday through Sunday 1:00 to 5:00 P.M. (except major holidays). Admission: Free.

This modest regional history museum is dedicated to the preservation and interpretation of Union County history from prehistoric times through the homesteading era, including development of the Santa Fe Trail.

Clayton Historical Park (all ages)
Off North Third Street.

Let the kids blow off some steam in this small city park replete with swings, a jungle gym, and "dinosaurs."

Clayton Lake State Park (all ages)
12 miles north of Clayton via Highway 370; (505) 374–8808. Admission: $5.00 for the day, $10.00 for overnight.

The amazing dinosaur "trackway" features more than 500 footprints of eight species of dinosaurs, including the flying pterodactyl and ancient crocodiles, left more than 100 million years ago. It's best to view the tracks in the morning and the late afternoon. The park

Folsom **Man**

One group of people who probably saw activity in the Capulin Volcano have never been discovered, but evidence of them has. In 1908 a cowboy and former slave, George McJunkin, discovered some spearpoints among bleached human bones in what was called Dead Horse Gulch (which should have been called Dead Mastodon Gulch), 8 miles west of Folsom. Folsom Man, based on the spearheads and mastodon skeletons found with him, dates back about 12,000 years. The Folsom July Jam takes place in downtown Folsom.

also offers swimming, boating, and camping facilities, and picnicking sites at the small lake (the result of a dam built in Cieneguilla—meaning "small marsh"—in 1955). There is also excellent trout, catfish, and bass fishing.

Kiowa National Grassland and Lake McClellan (all ages) 😎 Ⓐ 🤸
15 miles south of Clayton via Highway 402. Visitor center is in Clayton at 714 Main Street; (505) 374–9652. Admission and primitive camping are **free.**
Between Clayton and the Texas/Oklahoma border to the east, this vast area was once the site of many of the old homesteads of the famous Land Rush of the late 1800s. Farmers overworked their lands, raising crops, such as corn and wheat, that shouldn't have been grown there. Then, during the 1930s Great Dust Bowl, these farms had to be abandoned. Slowly the Department of Agriculture is replanting the area with native grass species. Cibola National Park manages the 136,000-acre park, which will never be farmed again. The prairie-fringed orchid, the prong-horned antelope, and the prairie chicken are some of the local attractions. There's even talk of reintroducing the bison.

At **Lake McClellan** there are campgrounds (developed and undeveloped), picnic areas, a visitor center, and water skiing (bring your own gear, though). This is frontier country, so bring plenty of food and supplies.

Where to Eat

Eklund Dining Room and Saloon.
15 Main Street; (505) 374–2551; www.the eklund.com. Built in 1892. Mexican and American fare. Children's menu. Open daily 11:00 A.M. to 9:00 P.M. $–$$

Hi-Ho Cafe. 1201 South First Street; (505) 374–9515. Family-style all-you-can-eat buffet and really big hamburgers! Open daily 5:00 A.M. to 8:00 P.M. $–$$

Rabbit Ear Cafe. 402 North First Street; (505) 374–9912. Mexican staples like enchiladas and burritos. Open Tuesday through Saturday 6:00 A.M. to 9:00 P.M. $–$$

Where to Stay

Kokopelli Lodge Best Western. 702 South First Street; (505) 374–2589. Fifty-one units with free hot breakfast buffet and cable television, outdoor pool, laundry facilities, sauna, and exercise room. Pets welcome (with small deposit). $$

Super 8 Motel. 1425 South First Street; (505) 374–8127. The motel offers thirty-one comfortable rooms with cable television. Shopping nearby. $–$$

For More Information

Chamber of Commerce. (505) 374–9253 or (800) 390–7858; www.claytonnew mexico.org.

Annual Community Events

SPRINGTIME
Dinosaur Daze. Downtown area; (505) 374–9253. An open-air bazaar featuring an Old West dance complete with costumes and old-fashioned dance prizes. Also a **free** tour of dinosaur tracks at Clayton Lake State Park.

FOURTH OF JULY
Rabbit Ear Roundup Rodeo. Union County Fairgrounds; (505) 374–9361. The community's largest celebration, including an arts and crafts show, dances, a rodeo, a barbecue, a street parade, and fireworks.

MID-AUGUST
Union County Fair. Union County Fairgrounds; (505) 374–9361. Livestock and agriculture exhibits, food, and music.

FIRST WEEKEND IN OCTOBER
Clayton Arts Festival. American Legion Hall, P.O. Box 562, Clayton 88415; (505) 374–9253. Fine arts, crafts, and purchase awards. You can buy art at a public showing through a bidding process known as "purchase awards." Art left unsold at the end of the day is "awarded" by jury to the highest bidder.

Southeast New Mexico

S outheast New Mexico is an area of stunning natural beauty and sparse population. Like many areas of the West and the Southwest, sometimes the sagebrush here outnumber the people! Nonetheless, there are some splendid sights to encounter in this corner of the state. Carlsbad Caverns is one of the wonders of the world, and you will marvel at its grandeur. The Mescalero Apache reservation near Alamogordo welcomes visitors to its vast and rich lands. Farther along, you can walk through the pretty town of Lincoln, where Billy the Kid hid during his last escape.

The kids will get a kick out of visiting Smokey Bear State Park in Capitán. They'll find out about the famous bear firsthand. If the extraterrestrial is your thing, then Roswell is an important stop. This is the site of the famous UFO sighting of 1947. People swear that aliens actually touched down for a visit!

Fort Sumner and Vicinity

US 60 at US 84.

The town grew out of the settlements around the fort, which was built in 1862 to protect the Bosque Redondo reservation. Later it was a major stop on the Goodnight-Loving cattle trail that stretched from Texas to Wyoming.

SOUTHEAST

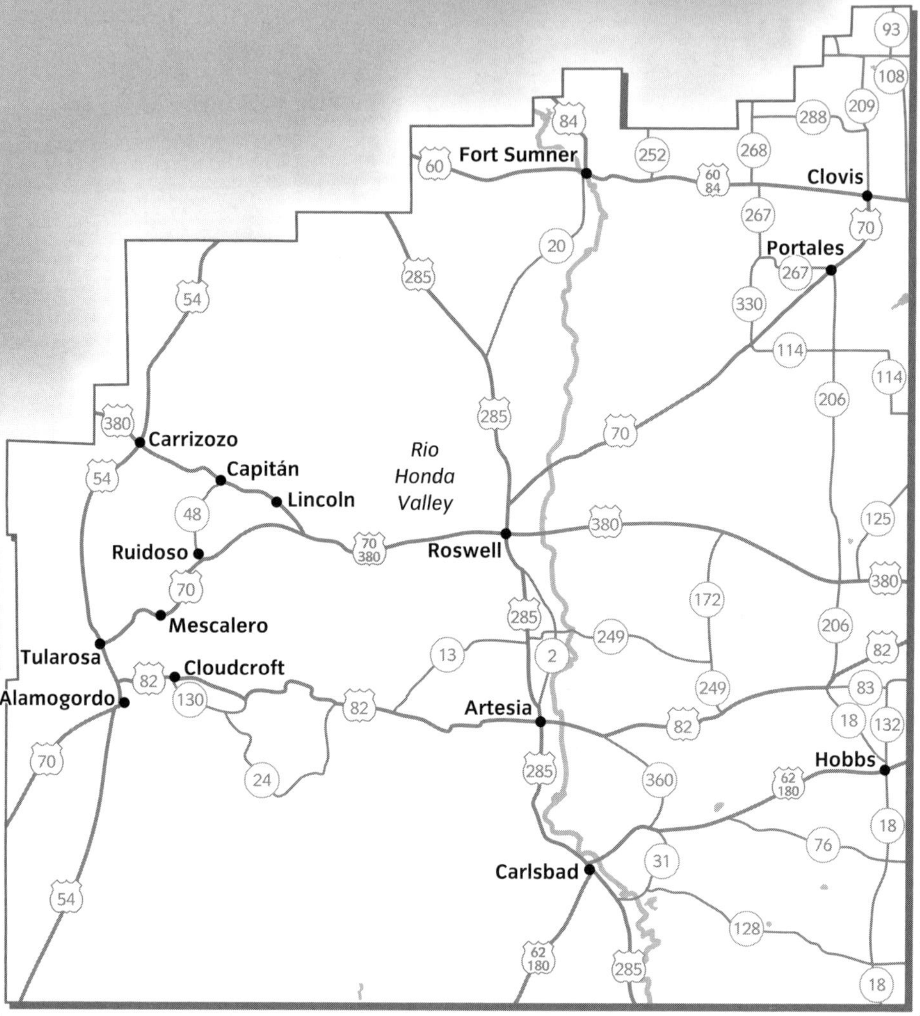

Fort Sumner
Clovis
Portales
Carrizozo
Capitán
Lincoln
Ruidoso
Mescalero
Tularosa
Cloudcroft
Alamogordo
Roswell
Artesia
Hobbs
Carlsbad

Rio Honda Valley

93
108
288 209
252 268
60
84
267
70
20
285
54
330
114
114
285
380
54
48
70
380
70
206
125
380
172
206
285
249
82
13
2
249
83
82
130
82
82
18 132
24
285
360
62
180
18
70
31
76
54
62
180
285
128
18

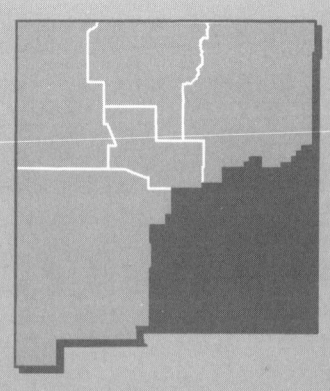

Billy the Kid Museum (all ages)

1601 East Sumner Avenue/US 60; (505) 355–2380 or (800) 556–7049; www.billythekid museumfortsumner.com. Open daily from 8:30 A.M. to 5:00 P.M.; closed on major holidays and from January 1 to 15. Admission: $4.00 for adults, $2.00 for kids 6–11.

This is a privately owned museum that has first-class displays of Billy the Kid memorabilia (like his rifle), as well as Indian artifacts, old-time buggies, and information about Fort Sumner. The children will be riveted by the wildness of the Wild West that Billy so perfectly embodied.

Fort Sumner State Monument (ages 10 to 12)

7 miles southeast of the town of Fort Sumner. Travel east on US 60/84, then south on Highway 212 (Billy the Kid Road); (505) 355–2573. Open Wednesday through Monday 8:30 A.M. to 5:00 P.M. Admission: $3.00 for adults, **free** for children 17 and under.

In the history of the development of the West, nothing is more tragic than the story of the Long Walk. More than 10,000 Navajo and Apache were herded off the lands their people had lived on for thousands of years, marched hundreds of miles across the desert, and incarcerated at Fort Sumner. The Indians endured disease and hunger here from 1863 to 1868, when shortages of food and firewood forced the government to let them go. The ruins of this old fort are important for the children to see. The visitor center has exhibits explaining this painful part of America's past.

A few yards away from the ruins of the fort is the Fort Sumner State Monument, a memorial to the Navajo and Apache who lived and died here. Fort Sumner's other claim to fame is the lore of Billy the Kid, whose real name was William Bonney. He is by far the main reason visitors come to this part of the state. This is where Pat Garrett killed Billy the Kid.

Old Fort Sumner Museum (all ages)

172 Billy the Kid Road; (505) 355–2942. Open daily 8:30 A.M. to 5:00 P.M. Admission: $3.50 for adults, $2.50 for children 7–14, children under 7 **free.**

Before you get to the site of the monument, you'll pass this privately owned museum, which is also headquarters for the Billy the Kid Outlaw Gang, Inc., an organization devoted to preserving the authenticity of the Billy the Kid story. Billy the Kid (among others) is buried in the cemetery that separates the museum from Fort Sumner State Monument. The grave marker, encased in iron, has a history of being stolen and returned numerous times. Your kids may enjoy learning about the adventures of both Billy and his gravestone, as well as reading letters written by Billy the Kid. There's also a mural depicting Billy's story.

Fort **Sumner**

For more details on Billy the Kid, see the introduction to Lincoln.

Annual **Community Events**

SECOND WEEK OF JUNE
Old Fort Days Celebration. Downtown Fort Sumner; (505) 355–7705. Music festival, Billy the Kid drama, rodeo, parade, and good food.

Sumner Lake State Park (all ages)
US 84 and Highway 203, 16 miles north of Fort Sumner; (505) 355–2541. Admission: $5.00 for the day, $10.00 for overnight (extra $4.00 with hookup).

This area has developed and primitive campsites with eighteen electricity hookups. The park includes a large lake formed by a dam along the Pecos River. The lake irrigates the farms along the river, but fishing is what draws visitors, especially in May, when the walleye are jumping onto your hooks. No visitor center, marina, or trails here (everything else, though).

Where to Eat

Dariland. 1304 Sumner Avenue; (505) 355–2337. Good sandwiches and ice cream. $

Fred's Restaurant and Lounge. 1408 East Sumner Avenue; (505) 355–7500. Mexican and American food, but especially known for its "conquistador" burrito. Open Monday through Friday 11:00 A.M. to 9:00 P.M. $$

Where to Stay

The Coronado. 309 West Sumner Avenue; (505) 355–2466. Here you'll find fifteen rooms and a nearby restaurant and laundry. $

Billy the Kid Country Inn. 1700 East Sumner Avenue; (505) 355–7414. The inn has nineteen rooms and a restaurant and laundry nearby. $

For More Information

Chamber of Commerce. 707 North Fourth Street, (505) 355–7705; www.ftsumner chamber.com.

Roswell

U.S. Highway 380.

Whatever you think you know about UFOs, think again, because this town is already ahead of you. Back in 1947, a year of an incredible number of UFO sightings all over New Mexico, a spacecraft supposedly crash-landed here. People found strange debris on a farm outside town and what they thought was the detritus of a spaceship. Ever since then, Roswell has been the focus of hundreds of newspaper articles, radio and television programs, and books as investigators try to uncover the "real" facts. To honor its history, the city holds the **Roswell UFO Festival** every July.

International UFO Museum and Research Center (ages 10 to 12)
114 North Main; (505) 625–9495; www.iufomrc.org. Open daily 9:00 A.M. to 5:00 P.M. Admission: Free.

This museum is run by a man named Walter Haut, who was a public relations officer for the Roswell Army Air Field. It was Haut who claimed that he knew the army had collected what was thought to be an alien spacecraft. The army claimed it was a downed weather balloon. Haut maintains otherwise. The kids will love visiting this modest nonprofit museum to find out the story for themselves.

Roswell Museum and Art Center (ages 10 to 12)
100 West Eleventh Street (at Main Street); (505) 624–6744; www.roswellmuseum.org. Open Monday through Saturday 9:00 A.M. to 5:00 P.M., Sunday 1:00 to 5:00 P.M. Admission: Free.

If your kids laugh at the idea of a UFO, then you can take them on a more serious excursion into reality. This museum has a special area dedicated to Robert H. Goddard, the "father of rocket science." There is a replica of Goddard's original science laboratory, where he worked from 1930 to 1942 developing the first liquid-fuel rockets. There's a planetarium, too. While the kids get a perspective on early rocket ships, the grown-ups can wander through the Art Center portion of this small complex and see the largest collection of Peter Hurd paintings in the Southwest.

Spring River Park and Zoo (all ages)
College Boulevard and Atkinson Avenue, 1 mile north of Roswell; (505) 624–6760. Open year-round from 10:00 A.M. to sunset during the warmer months of the year; winter hours vary, so call ahead. Rides are open Wednesday through Sunday through the summer 1:00 to 6:00 P.M. Admission: Free (25 cents for rides).

This is a children's paradise. First, there's the zoo, featuring buffalo and elk and a petting zoo. There are also a delightful prairie dog town, a fishing lake open only to children, a playground with a carousel and miniature train that offers rides, and picnic facilities. You might find it fun to take along a picnic and a good book to read—while the children are fishing and watching the prairie dogs, you'll have something to do, too!

Bitter Lake National Wildlife Refuge (all ages)

US 380, 13 miles east of Roswell or 10 miles northeast on US 285; (505) 622–6755. Open a ½ hour before sunrise to a ½ hour after sunset, daily.

This is the winter refuge for migratory waterfowl, especially the least tern. It's also where cranes winter by the tens of thousands, along with hundreds of geese and ducks. You can't camp here, but you can take the kids with a picnic, field glasses, and camera and wander along the well-marked routes and paths, or take an 8-mile self-guided driving tour on the southern end to observe the wildlife. Late autumn and winter are best for sight-seeing.

Bottomless Lakes State Park (all ages)

US 380 and Highway 409, 16 miles southeast of Roswell; (505) 624–6058. Admission: $5.00 for the day, $10.00 for overnight (extra $4.00 with hookup).

Another waterfowl hangout, once upon a time it was a pit stop for the Goodnight-Loving cattle trail. Now its graceful scenic beauty with lakes dotted throughout the park gives the visitor a peaceful spot to camp, bird-watch, and swim.

Where to Eat

Hungry American Family Restaurant. 3012 North Main; (505) 622–1266. A good place for American-country food. $$–$$$

Julie's Place. 1704 South Union Avenue; (505) 625–8776. Good green chile cheese-burgers and enchiladas. Open Monday through Saturday 8:00 A.M. to 7:00 P.M. $–$$

Nuthin' Fancy Cafe. 2103 North Main Street; (505) 623–4098. Home-cooked American food, plus soups and salads. Open daily 6:00 A.M. to 9:00 P.M. $–$$

Where to Stay

Budget Inn. 220 West Second Street; (505) 623–3811. Forty-two comfortable rooms fill the inn, as well as a small pool. There is a restaurant nearby. $

Frontier Motel. 3010 North Main Street; (505) 622–1400. The motel has thirty-eight remodeled rooms. **Free** continental breakfast. Outdoor pool. Restaurants nearby. $

Ramada Inn. 2803 West Second Street; (505) 623–9440. The inn offers one hundred large rooms, hot tub, **free** continental breakfast, and restaurant on site. $$

For More Information

Chamber of Commerce. 131 West Second Street; (505) 623–5695 or (877) 849–7679; www.roswellnm.org.

Visitor's Bureau. (505) 624–7704; (888) ROSWELL; www.roswell.cvb.com.

Lincoln

US 380, 12 miles east of Capitán.

Lincoln is a charming, old-time village so perfectly preserved that the entire town is on the National Register of Historic Places. Despite its modern-day prettiness, however, once this was a Wild West hamlet where there were shoot-'em-ups aplenty. Billy the Kid got his start here while working as part of the private militia of a local merchant, the Englishman John Tunstall. Billy idolized Tunstall. When the merchant was ambushed and murdered one day in 1878, Billy went on the warpath, gunning down everyone he thought had been a part of the dirty deed. For three days the guns didn't stop, until Sheriff Pat Garrett came to town to bring some order. He and a posse captured Billy at Stinking Rock Ranch, but not for long. Billy escaped back to Lincoln and hid. But Garrett finally flushed him out in the barn of a rich landowner, Lucien Maxwell, and shot him dead. The site of the shooting (and Billy's grave) is at Fort Sumner. These gun battles became known as the Lincoln County Wars. This is a slice of history that your kids will eat up. They can trace Billy's path around town and check out the important sites of the famous battles for themselves. Actually, the whole town constitutes the Lincoln State Monument. At the historical center, you can buy a pass for $6.00 that gets you and the family into every site of the monument.

Lincoln County Visitor Center and Museum (all ages)
US 380; (505) 653–4025. Open daily 8:30 A.M. to 4:30 P.M.

Find out everything you and your family would ever want to know about Billy the Kid, the Lincoln County Wars, the cowboys of that era, the Apaches who lived in and around Lincoln County, and the famous buffalo soldiers—the black cavalry of the U.S. Army.

John Tunstall's Big Mercantile Shop (all ages)
US 380; (505) 653–4049. Open daily 9:00 A.M. to 4:30 P.M. Admission: $6.00 for adults, free for children under 17.

Another great stop for the kids, it is also the local courthouse and a museum with displays of life in Lincoln in the 1880s.

Annual Community Events

EARLY AUGUST
Old Lincoln Days. Downtown; (505) 653–4372. The town re-creates the Lincoln County Wars as well as Billy the Kid's last escape. It's usually packed with visitors and has a jolly, festive atmosphere your kids will really enjoy.

Where to Eat

Isaac's Table at the Ellis Store Country Inn. Downtown Lincoln; (800) 653–6460. Fine continental cuisine. Open Wednesday through Saturday for dinner only. $$$

Wortley Hotel. US 380; (505) 653–4300. The hotel restaurant serves old-fashioned food, in the style of the 1880s. Open Wednesday through Sunday for breakfast and lunch from 8:00 A.M. to 2:00 P.M. and for dinner at 6:00 P.M. by reservation. $–$$

Where to Stay

Casa de Patron Bed and Breakfast. Highway 380 East; (505) 653–4676. www.casa patron.com. $$–$$$

Wortley Hotel. US 380; (505) 653–4300. If you want to round out your dip into first-class Wild West history, then a stay at this hotel could be a lot of fun. Owned once by Pat Garrett and now by the Museum of New Mexico, all seven rooms are decorated in 1880s frontier style. $$

Capitán

US 380 at Highway 48.

This is Smokey Bear country. The town of Capitán is the birthplace and burial site of the famous symbol of forest-fire prevention. This is a great stop for the kids. They've seen the ads on TV; they've seen Smokey on the bulletin boards at school; now they can see where it all began.

In 1950 a man-made fire nearly destroyed the Lincoln National Forest. Firefighters managed to save a bear cub whose paws were badly burned. The bear was flown to Santa Fe to be helped. When he healed, the rangers named him Smokey and used a cartoon pic-

Annual **Community Events**

EARLY AUGUST
Lincoln County Fair. County Fairgrounds; (505) 653–4372. Rodeo, juried livestock show, art, crafts, and food.

ture of him to bring forest-fire awareness to a generation of children and their families. Public service announcements featuring Smokey have brought this awareness to new generations.

Smokey Bear Historical Park (all ages)
118 Smokey Bear Boulevard; (505) 354–2748. Open daily from 9:00 A.M. to 5:00 P.M. Admission: $2.00 for adults, $1.00 for children 7–12, under 7 **free.**

The visitor center tells a bit of the Smokey Bear story. There are also artifacts from the area.

Smokey Bear Museum and Shop (all ages)
102 Smokey Bear Boulevard; (505) 354–2298. Open daily from 9:00 A.M. to 4:00 P.M. Admission: $2.00 for adults, children under 12 **free.**

This log cabin museum houses exhibits on the Smokey Bear lore and memorabilia. Kids can pore through the museum's scrapbooks about Smokey. They can press a button and hear a larger-than-life replica of Smokey speak to them then wander through a wonderful collection of Smokey Bear toys and books. Most of the memorabilia dates from the 1950s and early 1960s. It will certainly stir up your memories and probably encourage questions from your kids about your life in the "olden days."

Smokey Bear **Stampede**

Check out the **Smokey Bear Stampede,** a rodeo, barbecue, Western dance, and parade, with Smokey front and center. Held on the Fourth of July. Call (505) 354–2273 for more information.

Where to Eat

Smokey Bear Restaurant in the Smokey Bear Motel. Smokey Bear Boulevard; (505) 354–2253. Good American-country fare in a child-friendly atmosphere. Open 7:00 A.M. to 8:00 P.M. $–$$

Where to Stay

Smokey Bear Motel. Smokey Bear Boulevard; (505) 354–2253. Motor lodge is equipped with microwaves and refrigerators in every room. Laundry facilities just a block away. $–$$

For More Information

Chamber of Commerce. (505) 354–2273.

Ruidoso

U.S. Highway 70.

Located on what was once the Chisum Trail in the Sacramento Mountains, Ruidoso (meaning "noisy"—after the chattering stream nearby) is one of New Mexico's leading playgrounds.

Hubbard Museum of the American West (all ages)

841 Highway 70 West; (505) 378–4142; www.hubbardmuseum.com. Open daily from 9:00 A.M. to 5:00 P.M. Admission: $6.00 for adults, $2.00 for children 6–16, free for children under 6.

Visiting Ruidoso means seeing horses, but even if you don't bet and horse races don't interest you, it's still fascinating to explore the racing oval, the stalls, and the museum. The museum displays more than 10,000 items relating to the horse, from saddlery to surreys-with-the-fringe-on-top, and is a great place to take the kids.

Lincoln County Overland Stagecoach Company (all ages)

(505) 653–4954. Admission: $30 for adults (long ride), $15 for children 3–16; $15 for adults (short ride), $10 for children.

Your family might enjoy someone else driving for a change—and you'll learn some history, to boot! This family-owned stagecoach company offers long and short rides. The longer,

Quarter Horse **Futurity**

The richest horse race (the purse is $2 million) in the United States, the Quarter Horse Futurity is run each Labor Day at the Ruidoso Downs.

Rio Hondo **Valley**

Both Ruidoso and Lincoln are in the beautiful Rio Hondo Valley, an area full of orchards, horse farms, and gorgeous grazing lands. A drive on US 70 to the south of Lincoln brings you and your family right through the whole valley. If your family enjoys touring an art community, stop in **San Patricio,** home to the late Henrietta Wyeth and other artists. In any case, enjoy the drive and plan on a picnic.

5.5-mile ride lasts about an hour and a half and kicks off with a historical talk about stagecoaches before meandering through the Lincoln County countryside along the Ozanne Trail to Feather Cave, Fort Stanton, Angel's Crossing, and an old cemetery. The shorter ride visits many of the same sights but lasts about forty minutes.

Where to Eat

Casa Blanca. 501 Mechem Drive; (505) 257–2495. Mexican/Southwestern, but with American fare, too. Children's menu. Open Monday through Thursday 11:00 A.M. to 8:00 P.M., until 10:00 P.M. on weekends. $–$$

Cattle Baron Steak and Seafood. 657 Sudderth Drive; (505) 257–9355. Elegant but friendly. Children's menu. In the summertime, sit by the indoor waterfall. Open Sunday through Thursday 11:30 A.M. to 9:00 P.M., until 10:00 P.M. on weekends. $–$$

Where to Stay

Bestway Inn. 2052 Highway 70 (at junction with SR 48); (505) 378–8000. $–$$

Dan Dee Cabins Resort. 310 Main Road; (505) 257–2165 or (800) 345–4848. Cottages in the woods at 7,000 feet above sea level. $$.

Days Inn. 2088 Highway 70 (near junction with SR 48); (505) 378–4299. $–$$

Holiday Inn Express. 400 Highway 70, after junction with Sudderth Drive; (505) 257–3736. $$

Shadow Mountain Lodge. 107 Main Road. (505) 257–4886 or (800) 441–4331. All rooms have fireplaces. No pets. $$

Other Things **to Do (all ages)**

- Sledding/inner tubing at **Winter Park.** North on Highway 48, just west on Ski Run Road; (505) 336–7079

- Trout pond fishing at **Seeping Springs.** 4 miles east of Ruidoso on US 70; (505) 378–4216

- Go-karting, miniature golf, and bumper boats at **Funtrackers.** 101 Carrizo Canyon Road; (505) 257–3275

- Horseback riding at **Grindstone Stables,** 523 Resort Drive, (505) 257–2241, and at **Cowboys' Stables,** at 1027 North Lands Road off US 70, (505) 378–8217. The Ruidoso Visitor Center has other stable choices.

- **Flying J Ranch,** a little Western town on Ski Run Road set up in the summer. The fun starts at 6:00 P.M. with pony rides and a "shoot-out." Then you are served a chuck wagon dinner (around 7:30 P.M.) with good and wholesome entertainment offered until 8:00 P.M. or so; (505) 336–4330 or (888) 458–3595; www.flyingjranch.com.

For More Information

Chamber of Commerce/Visitor Bureau.
(505) 257–7395 or (877) RUIDOSO;
www.ruidoso.net.

Carrizozo and White Oaks Ghost Town

US 54 at US 380. White Oaks Ghost Town is 12 miles north of Carrizozo on US 54 and Highway 349; (505) 648–2732.

Once upon a time this was a wild and woolly mining town that grew up around the North Homestake mine. In its heyday in the 1870s, the mine seemed like a bottomless well of gold—over half a million dollars' worth of the stuff was extracted from here. White Oaks's population swelled to 4,000 at one point and became a haven for unsavory characters like cattle rustlers, outlaws, and women of easy virtue, as well as con artists of every stripe. Billy the Kid made a pit stop here once or twice. Eventually the mine played out, the new railroad links bypassed the town, and the ghosts took over. Now all you and your children will see are abandoned buildings, a plain historical marker, a cemetery, and one or two hardy residents who've braved the empty streets and decided to live here. In a wooden shack once known as ¡the old post office," there's a museum and a bar where you and the kids can get something to drink and pick through the displays and artifacts of a life long passed.

The town is named for the carrizozo reed grass native to the area.

Valley of Fires Recreation Area (all ages)

US 380, 3 miles west of Carrizozo; (505) 648–2241. Admission: $5.00 for the day, $7.00 for overnight ($11.00 extra with hookups).

For a special picnic site, you and your family couldn't find a better place than this recreation area, administered by the Bureau of Land Management. You'll find one of the youngest and most perfectly preserved lava flows in the United States. About 1,500 years ago a volcano called Little Black Peak erupted near here, spewing its molten rock some 44 miles across the landscape. By the time it had finished its work, the fiery outpouring had covered 172 square miles. What was left behind for us to see today is a series of 15-foot wavelike outcroppings rippling across the desert. Sprinkled throughout these hillocks of lava are prickly pear cacti so big they look like green saucers.

You and the kids can take a marker-guided walk through this volcanic wonderland then stop to have a picnic among the covered tables and playgrounds nearby. If you prefer to camp and spend a day or two exploring the area, there are twenty-five sites, some with electricity and water.

Tularosa

US 54.

Tularosa, the "City of Roses," is a small, pretty, typical New Mexican hamlet that was established after the Rio Grande flooded the town of Mesilla in 1860. There's an old adobe mission church along the highway. The Franciscans built it so that, once they converted the Apache, the Indians could attend Mass.

Three Rivers Petroglyph National Recreation Site (all ages)
On US 54, about 15 miles north of Tularosa.

You can't miss this well-marked site as you drive along US 54. Your kids will love walking the 3D 4-mile path looking for the more than 5,000 petroglyphs in this area. Petroglyphs are the carved drawings that ancient Native American peoples left behind as they moved from place to place. All of them are cut into the rocks. Some are markers directing other travelers, but you'll also be able to pick out animals, clouds, lightning bolts, and faces. Kids have a lot of fun deciphering the drawings.

Where to Eat

Al-O-Mar Restaurant. 205 Central Avenue; (505) 585–2129. Mexican and New Mexican food. Open daily 6:00 A.M. to 9:00 P.M. $–$$

Lazy DR Restaurant. Highway 470; (505) 585–2532. Good Mexican-American food. Open daily 6:00 A.M. to 9:00 P.M. $–$$

Where to Stay

Knotty Pine Motel. 355 Central Avenue; (505) 585–2199. $–$$

For More Information

Alamogordo Chamber of Commerce. (505) 437–6120.

Annual **Community Events**

MOTHER'S DAY
St. Francis de Paula Fiesta. St. Francis de Paula Church at 303 Encino; (505) 585–2793. Commemorating the victory of the 1868 battle against the Mescalero Apaches, which protected the town from further attacks. A queen is crowned, and there are traditional games, food, and music.

Mescalero Apache Reservation

Along US 70, 16 miles east of Tularosa.

By Southwestern standards, this reservation is small—"only" 460,000 acres. The Native Americans who live here are the descendants of the nomadic tribes that migrated south about 1,000 years ago and made their way to what is now New Mexico. They were permanently moved to this area by the U.S. government in 1873. Now they raise cattle and horses and make their teepees with evergreens instead of mescal cactus.

Ski Apache (all ages)
SR 532; (505) 336–4356. Snow report: (505) 257–9001.

Ski Apache is owned and operated by the Apache and features fifty-two runs and ten chairlifts. The slopes can accommodate 15,000 skiers.

For More Information

Mescalero Cultural Center. (505) 464–1270.

Alamogordo

US 54 at US 70.

By Southwestern standards, Alamogordo is a fairly large city of 30,000 people. Its name means "fat cottonwood." The town, founded in 1898, was another railroad stop for those on the move west. It got bigger when it was chosen as the site for Holloman Air Force Base and the White Sands Missile Range. Nowadays skiers pour in to tackle the trails in the Sacramento Mountains. There are lots of family activities in the area.

Alameda Park Zoo (all ages)
1321 North White Sands Boulevard; (505) 439–4290. Open daily except Christmas and New Year's Day, 9:00 A.M. to 5:00 P.M. Admission: $2.20 for adults, $1.10 for children under 11.

A visit to this zoo is one of those nice things to do in town. The Alameda is not a big-city animal display—it's a small, very old zoo. The railroad began displaying live animals here back in 1898 to amuse passengers during the long refueling stopover. It is very much a child-oriented place, where kids can feed the ducks and watch the coyotes loll in the sun.

Toy Train Depot (all ages)

1991 North White Sands Boulevard at Routes 54 and 70 (next to the zoo); (505) 437–2855; www.toytraindepot.homestead.com. Open Wednesday through Sunday noon to 4:30 P.M. Admission: $3.00.

Take the kids to see this turn-of-the-twentieth-century depot, where they get to take train rides around the park and look at hundreds of trains and thousands of feet of toy train setups.

Space Center (all ages)

End of Highway 2001: US 70 to Indian Wells Road, then north on Scenic Road, first right is Highway 2001; (505) 437–2840 or (877) 333–6589; www.spacefame.org. Center is open daily from 9:00 A.M. to 5:00 P.M. (except Christmas Day). Includes the International Space Hall of Fame Museum (admission: $2.50 for adults, $2.00 for children 4–12, children 3 and under **free**), the Clyde W. Tombaugh Space Theater (planetarium in museum and OmniMax system next door; fees range from $4.50 to $6.50), the Stapp Air and Space Park, and the Shuttle Camp.

This is, by far, one of the biggest attractions in the area. It is a striking edifice tucked into the foothills of the mountains. You can't miss the radiant gold building and its 90-foot white rocket.

This is a place set up to appeal to both parents and children. The planetarium has shows every two hours, with a rotating OmniMax movie program and a laser light presentation. On weekends you and your family can get a ticket that gets you into all three events.

The museum houses displays recognizing both the American and Soviet space programs and features full-scale replicas of rockets. Outdoors, there's a reentry module in the Rocket Garden. The kids can play space flight to their hearts' content. You might even be interested in sending your children to the Space Center Shuttle Program that the museum runs each summer. Children from third through ninth grades can spend a week at the camp enjoying hands-on activities relating to the shuttle program. There's a concession stand in the gift shop of the museum.

National Solar Observatory (ages 10 to 12)

Sacramento Mountain, U.S. Highway 82 east to Highway 24 South; (505) 434–7000; www.sunspot.noao.edu. Guided tours Saturday, Memorial Day to Labor Day, or self-guided during the week.

The work of this observatory is to monitor weather patterns that relate to the movement of sunspots. As you wind your way through the mountains, take a break and enjoy the gorgeous views. Be sure to pack a picnic lunch, because there are no eating facilities here.

White Sands National Monument (all ages)

US 70/82, 15 miles southwest of Alamogordo; (505) 479–6124; www.nps.gov/whsa. Open daily. Admission: $3.00 for adults 17 and older, **free** for children 16 and under. Visitor center and museum. Moonlight bike tours: $5.00 for adults, $2.50 for children under 16. Advance registration is required; call (505) 679–2599, extension 111.

White Sands Missile Range and Trinity Site

US 380 southeast of Socorro; (505) 437–6120 or (800) 826–0294. Open twice a year, for special tours only, on the first Saturday of April and October. Reservations are required. This is the site of the first atomic bomb detonation in July 1945. It is located in the middle of a barren desert and is one of the more famous (or infamous) places in New Mexico. It can be an instructive visit for the kids if your vacation coincides with the tour dates.

This is one of those amazing wonders of the world that you can't believe is in your own country. At nearly 300 square miles wide and 30 to 40 feet high, it is the largest gypsum dune field in the world. Several million years ago this was a lakebed. When the earth's atmosphere changed all those eons past and the lake dried up, the gypsum sand was left behind. Shifting winds cause changing ripples in the topography, adding to the grandeur of this natural phenomenon. In the summer it's just too hot to do anything here, but take the 8-mile loop drive. If you go in autumn or winter, the kids can bring their snowboards or plastic sheet sleds and fly across the dunes. Another way to see the dunes is on a moonlit night when they are transformed into a magical moonscape. In fact, park rangers hold moonlight bicycle tours and campfires during the full moon. It's remarkable territory you'll want to remember. Bring a camera—the kids can take photos to school for show-and-tell.

Dog Canyon and Oliver Lee Memorial State Park (all ages) Ⓐ Ⓧ Ⓕ
US 54, 10 miles south at Dog Canyon; (505) 437–8284. Open year-round. Admission: $5.00 entrance fee, $10.00 overnight ($4.00 for hookups).

If you've seen enough of the big sites and want to spend a few days in the cool of the forests, then head out to the homesite of the first white settler in the area—a man named Frenchy. Camping here is great for both you and the kids. It's quiet and cool, with views of White Sands. For the dinosaur nuts in the family, a short trail takes you to an overlook where you can see a rare dinosaur trail of sorts containing more than 500 footprints.

There are historical exhibits, too, which detail the history of the Apache occupation of Dog Canyon and the Sacramento Mountains even as it was used as a primary water source by Oliver Lee's Circle Cross cattle range.

Lincoln National Forest (all ages)

Accessible by US 70/380 and US 82; (505) 434–7200. Developed campgrounds (showers and toilets) are available from May through October. RV sites (no hookups) with dump stations. Primitive camping year-round. Fees: $9.00–$11.00 for camping.

A vast wilderness of nature trails, campgrounds, forests, and woodlands. If you decide to take the family here, you should know that there are no formal recreational facilities such as swimming or boating—just woodland trails and a lot of you and nature getting along together. You may want to take along games, etc., for the kids to enjoy at night.

Annual **Community Events**

MID-MAY
Saturday in the Park. Washington Park; (505) 439–4142. Arts and crafts, with Holloman Air Force Base demonstrations.

JUNE
Flight Fest. Space Center; (505) 437–2840. An amateur model rocket competition.

LABOR DAY WEEKEND
Cottonwood Festival. Alameda Park; (505) 437–6120. A juried and nonjuried arts event with food and entertainment.

SEPTEMBER
International Space Hall of Fame Induction. Space Center; (505) 437–2840. Contributors to space research and exploration are honored in this yearly ceremony.

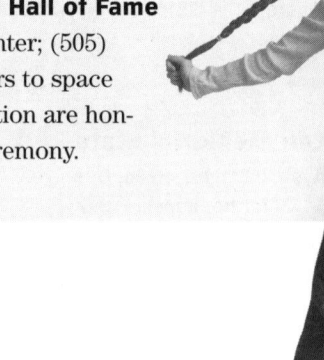

Where to Eat

Ramona's. 2913 North White Sands Boulevard; (505) 437–7616. Good Mexican food. Open Monday through Saturday 6:00 A.M. to 10:00 P.M., Sunday 7:00 A.M. until 10:00 P.M. $–$$

Where to Stay

Alamo. 1450 North White Sands Boulevard; (505) 437–1000. $–$$

Best Western. 1021 South White Sands Boulevard; (505) 437–2110. $–$$

Holiday Inn. 1401 South White Sands Boulevard; (505) 437–7100. $$

Motel 6. 251 Panorama Boulevard; (505) 434–5970. $–$$

For More Information

Chamber of Commerce. 1301 North White Sands Boulevard; (505) 437–6120 or (800) 826–0294; www.alamogordo.com.

Cloudcroft

US 82, 17 miles east of US 54.

Getting to Cloudcroft ("cloud in a croft," or meadow) is a beautiful experience because the kids get to see the radical topographical changes typical of New Mexico. You start out on the desert floor, then climb 5,000 feet to the summit of the Sacramento Mountains, where the vegetation changes to the pines and bushes of the high mountain range. It's an entertaining game getting the kids to spot the differences and write them down. (Cloudcroft is nearly 10,000 feet above sea level, so be sure to bring plenty of warm sweaters and jackets; even in the summer it can get quite chilly when you least expect it.)

Once a thriving logging town, Cloudcroft is now famous as a resort and recreation center.

Sacramento Mountains Historical Society Museum (ages 10 to 12)
1000 US 82; (505) 682–2932. **Open Monday, Tuesday, Friday, and Saturday 10:00 A.M. to 4:00 P.M., Sunday 1:00 to 4:00 P.M. Admission: $3.00 for adults, $1.00 for children.**

Located in a restored pioneer log cabin, the museum houses turn-of-the-twentieth-century memorabilia.

Mexican Canyon **Trestle**

This breathtaking bridge, built in 1899, is all that remains of the spur built by the El Paso and Northeastern Railroad. Located just 1 mile west of Cloudcroft.

Annual **Community Events**

MEMORIAL DAY WEEKEND
Mayfair. Zenith Park; (505) 682–2733. Juried arts and crafts fair; along with a hayride, horseshoe competition, square dances, food, and guided nature trail walks.

JUNE
Western Roundup. Zenith Park; (505) 682–2733. Old-time fiddling contests, a pie auction, Western street dances, and a Mexican-style rodeo.

Bluegrass Festival. Zenith Park; (505) 687–3520. Bluegrass and gospel groups from southern New Mexico and west Texas perform all weekend long.

WEEKEND CLOSEST TO THE FOURTH OF JULY
July Jamboree. Zenith Park; (505) 682–2733. Arts and crafts, hayrides, horseshoe tournaments, and food.

FIRST FULL WEEKEND IN OCTOBER
Cloudcroft Oktoberfest. Zenith Park; (505) 682–2733. This is the largest arts and crafts fair in town.

LATE OCTOBER
Harvest Fest. Downtown; (505) 682–2733. Hayrides, pumpkin-carving contests, and lots of other kids' activities.

MID-DECEMBER
Christmas in Cloudcroft. Zenith Park; (505) 682–2733. The best time to really enjoy Cloudcroft is during Christmas. The kids would love a visit during this time. There's a huge parade, with Santa leading the way, plus a very funny pet parade. Mrs. Santa has her own kitchen behind the Chamber of Commerce and hands out free cookies and hot drinks. There's a live nativity scene with a bonfire, an ice sculpture contest, light tours, and Christmas carols performed in the park.

Karr Canyon (all ages)
US 82, 8 miles west of Cloudcroft.
A good spot to enjoy bird-watching.

Bluff Springs (all ages)
Highway 6563, 14 miles south of Cloudcroft.
A prime viewing area for warblers, hummingbirds, and wild turkeys.

Sunspot Solar **Observatory**

The **Sunspot Solar Observatory** on NM 6563, 18 miles south of Cloudcroft (505-434-7190), can teach your kids how scientists monitor the sun's activity. There are guided tours (daily during the summer at 2:00 P.M.; free) as well as selfguided tours. Open daily 10:00 A.M. to 6:00 P.M.

Where to Eat

Rebecca's Lounge. 1 Corona Place; (505) 682–2566 or (800) 395–6343. This tasty, casual restaurant is located in the Lodge (see below) and is open for breakfast, lunch, and dinner.

Where to Stay

The Lodge. 1 Corona Place; (505) 682– 2566 or (800) 395–6343; www.thelodgeresort.com. The only hotel/dining spot in Cloudcroft, it has an alpine style with cozy fires going summer and winter. It has a venerable past: In bygone years people like Judy Garland and Clark Gable stayed here. Today its atmosphere is relaxed and casual. $$$

For More Information

Chamber of Commerce. (505) 682–2733; www.cloudcroft.net.

Carlsbad and Vicinity

US 285 at US 62/180.

This part of Pecos River country has a lot for the family to do.

Carlsbad Museum and Art Center (all ages)

418 West Fox Street; (505) 887–0276. Open Monday through Saturday 10:00 A.M. to 5:00 P.M. Admission: **Free.**

If the caverns inspire thoughts of dinosaurs and ancient lands in your children, then this museum is a fun place to go, with its mixture of mammoth bones, Indian artifacts, and cowboy paraphernalia.

Brantley Lake State Park (all ages)

County Road 30 off US 285, 12 miles north of Carlsbad; (505) 457–2384. Admission: $5.00 per day per vehicle ($10.00 for overnight plus $4.00 for hookups). No marina.

When indoor activities start to tire your children, take them to the lake. The lake was created when part of the Pecos River was dammed. The view from the top of the dam is spectacular. If the kids have never been near a real dam, this trip is interesting just for that. The lake itself is wonderful but is still in the process of being developed. At present, your kids can see cranes, sparrows, and owls. There's a kite-flying rally in March and a Kid's Fishing Clinic in May, as well as special Saturday night campground programs held throughout the summer.

Living Desert State Park (all ages)

Skyline Drive just off Route 285 North at the northwestern edge of Carlsbad; (505) 887–5516. Open daily 8:00 A.M. to 8:00 P.M. In the winter, closes at 5:00 P.M. Closed Christmas Day. Admission: $5.00 for adults, $3.00 for children 7–12, children 6 and under **free.**

Another great place to take the kids for a picnic and a stroll. The park is located at the top of the Ocotillo Hills. There's a 1.3-mile self-guided tour through the zoo (yes, another zoo!) that features a Mexican wolf, mountain lions, buffalo, bobcats, javelinas, and a botanical garden with some fascinating cactus plants.

Picnic **Spot**

Look for **Rattlesnake Springs Picnic Area** on Highway 418 between Carlsbad and the caverns for a quiet, cool place to enjoy a picnic lunch and do some bird-watching. Turkey vultures are plentiful here.

Paddle Wheel **Boat Trip**

A paddle wheel boat takes you cruising up and down the Pecos River. If your kids have never seen one of these glorious boats, this is worth the time. Available from May to September. Call (505) 887–0512 for more information.

Million Dollar Museum (all ages)

U.S. Highway 62/180, 20 miles south of Carlsbad on Main Street of White's City; (505) 785–2291. Open daily from 8:00 A.M. to 9:00 P.M. Admission: $3.00 for adults, $2.00 for children 6–12.

This is southwestern New Mexico's largest museum, and if someone in your family has a fascination with dolls, this is the place to go. This museum has more than ten rooms of dolls and doll accessories along with more Old West memorabilia.

Sitting Bull Falls (all ages)

US 285 North, 50 miles north of Carlsbad in the Lincoln National Forest. Turn west onto Highway 137 until the road forks. Take a right at County Road 409 for 8 miles; (505) 885–4181. Open year-round, sunrise to sunset. Sheltered picnic areas. Admission: $5.00 per vehicle (free on Wednesday).

This is a beautiful setting for a day of walking and picnicking in the heart of nature. It's a challenging drive but a delight once you get there.

Carlsbad Caverns National Park (ages 10 to 12)

US 62/180, approximately 25 miles south of Carlsbad at 3225 National Parks Highway; (505) 785–2232; www.nps.gov/cave. Ranger-guided tours are available. Admission: $6.00 per person 16 and over, $3.00 for ages 6 to 15, and ages 5 and under are free; individual cavern tours: $7.00 to $20.00.

A visit to Carlsbad Caverns puts you not only in the largest cavern in the United States but also in the company of bats—millions of Mexican freetail bats. In fact, bats are what enticed early settlers to have a look around here. What they found, in addition to these strange nocturnal creatures, was hundreds and hundreds of tons of guano, which they sold off to California orange growers as fertilizer.

Every year from May to October there are huge bat flights leaving the caverns at sunset and returning at dawn at a rate of 5,000 per minute. Park rangers are here each night during the season to explain bat habits.

In the caverns themselves there are two self-guided tours. One is an arduous 3-mile hike. The other has you descending to the floor of the cave in an elevator. Dress your family warmly even in the summer, and wear sturdy shoes to cope with the slippery paths.

Other Things to Do

New Cave (also known as Slaughter Canyon Cave). 23 miles south of the main caverns on Highway 418. Your kids may also enjoy the adventure of seeing this cave, although the trip is a bit of a challenge and is for the older members of the family only. Take US 62/180 to Highway 418, which turns into a rugged dirt road after 11 miles or so. You'll need to bring flashlights for everyone, water, hiking boots, and warm clothes—even in summer. This cave is an undeveloped natural wonder; you'll be taking a good mile hike just to get from the parking lot to the mouth of the cave. Strollers and baby backpacks are not allowed. It's an invigorating, Wild West experience.

Be sure to get your reservations in at the visitor center for the guided tours of the "King's Room" and "Queen's Room." They are the most memorable. If you have very young children, take advantage of the child care service, which allows parents to tour the caverns knowing the little ones are safely looked after.

Where to Eat

Church Street Grill. 301 West Church Street; (505) 885–3074. Burgers, burritos, and baskets. Open daily 7:00 A.M. to 8:00 P.M. $–$$

My Daddy's BBQ. 704 West Pierce Street; (505) 628–0196. Traditional barbecue smoked with hickory and mesquite. Open Monday through Friday 11:00 A.M. to 7:30 P.M., Saturday to 6:00 P.M. $$

Pizza Inn. 1210 West Pierce, (505) 887–7566; and 3005 National Parks Highway, (505) 887–5049. Open daily 11:00 A.M. to 11:00 P.M. $–$$

Where to Stay

Best Western Motel Stevens. 1829 South Canal Street; (505) 887–2851 or (800) 730–2851. The motel offers 222 rooms in a family atmosphere. Playground. Restaurant on premises. $$

Continental Inn. 3820 National Parks Highway; (505) 887–0341. Sixty rooms make up the inn. $–$$

Stagecoach Inn. 1819 South Canal Street; (505) 887–1148. Wading pool, playground, hot tub. Restaurant nearby. Laundry facilities. $

For More Information

Chamber of Commerce. 302 South Canal Street; (505) 887–6516 or (800) 221–1224; www.chamber.caverns.com.

Annual **Community Events**

MID-MAY
Mescal Roast. Living Desert State Park; (505) 887–5516. Traditional Mescalero Apache Indian ceremonies, mescal tastings, blessings, and dances.

JUNE
Carlsbad Western Week Celebration. Carlsbad Civic Center; (505) 887–6516. Return to the Old West with parades, rodeos, dancing in the street, and, of course, a barbecue.

SECOND THURSDAY IN AUGUST
Bat Flight Breakfast. At the Main Caverns; (505) 785–2232. Admission: $6.00 for adults, $3.00 for children 12 and under. Open 5:00 to 7:00 A.M. The rangers cook a big breakfast this morning and explain bat migrations while you and the kids wait for the "fly-in"—when the bats return to the caves by the thousands. After they return (and you've finished your breakfast), the rangers take you into the caverns to see the bats roosting. Your kids will never forget an experience like this (even if it is at dawn).

WEEKEND CLOSEST TO SEPTEMBER 16
September Sixteenth Celebration. San Jose Plaza; (505) 887–6516. Mexican rodeo and parades.

Hobbs

US 62/80 and Highway 18, 3 miles from the Texas border.

The town of Hobbs is in an area called the Llano Estacado (staked plain), which is a plateau of the High Plains desert that is itself a part of the Great Plains. This was the last area of the United States to be settled and was home to buffalo herds and native nomadic tribes for hundreds of years. The town was an important oil center after the "liquid gold" was discovered in 1928. Hobbs is also famous for its beef trade. Today it is mostly an industrial town.

Lea County Cowboy Hall of Fame (ages 10 to 12)

5317 Lovington Highway (on the campus of New Mexico Junior College); (505) 392–5518. Open Monday through Friday 10:00 A.M. to 5:00 P.M., Saturday 1:00 to 5:00 P.M. Admission: Free.

Hobbs and Lea Counties produce the most rodeo champions in the United States. The Hall of Fame celebrates the cowboy and the rodeo. There's also a pioneer kitchen and bedroom set up just as they would have been a century ago.

Maddox Lake (all ages)

Off US 62, 10 miles west of Hobbs.

For outdoor excitement for you and the children, there's Maddox Lake for fishing, as well as bird-watching for a variety of waterfowl.

Harry McAdams Park (all ages)

Off Highway 18 (Turner Street), 4 miles north of Hobbs; (505) 392–5845.

Closer to town, this park offers fifteen campsites with electric hookups. RVs can be accommodated (the pads are paved). There's a pond on the grounds where children can fish.

Annual **Community Events**

LATE SEPTEMBER

Staked Plains Roundup. Western Heritage Center at the Cowboy Hall of Fame; (505) 392–5518. Storytellers and "cowboy poets," western music, and rawhide braiding, among other shows of skill.

Where to Eat

Big Cheese Pizza. 2404 North Grimes; (505) 392–1520. Open daily 11:00 A.M. to 11:00 P.M. $–$$

Bovine and Swine's Barbecue Co. 2404 North Grimes; (505) 392–2800. Brisket and ribs. Open daily 11:00 A.M. to 9:00 P.M. $–$$

Ma Brown's Hamburgers. 1217 North Grimes; (505) 393–8129 and 321 East Main Street; (505) 393–7218. Open daily 10:30 A.M. to 9:00 P.M. $–$$

Where to Stay

Broadway Inn. 200 North Marland Boulevard; (505) 393–4101. Some of the seventy rooms have refrigerators and microwaves. Restaurant nearby. **Free** breakfast. $$

Days Inn. 211 North Marland Boulevard; (505) 397–6541. Fifty-seven contemporary rooms. Restaurant nearby. $–$$

Econo Lodge. 619 North Marland Boulevard; (505) 397–3591. The lodge offers thirty-eight modern rooms. **Free** breakfast. $

For More Information

Chamber of Commerce/Visitor Center. (505) 397–3202 or (800) 658–6291.

Portales

US 70, 19 miles southwest of Clovis.

Portales is a small, friendly college and farming town. Its academic environment comes from Eastern New Mexico University, and its farming wealth comes from peanuts—growing and processing them.

Blackwater Draw Archaeological Site and Museum (ages 10 to 12)

US 70 North and Highway 467, 7 miles northeast of Portales; (505) 562–2202. Open Monday through Saturday 10:00 A.M. to 5:00 P.M., Sunday noon to 5:00 P.M. (closed Monday in winter). Admission: $2.00 for adults, $1.00 for children 15 and under.

This is one of the most significant archaeological zones in the country and has only recently been opened to visitors. Your kids will learn all about the earliest human existence in the New World. Discovered in 1932, this was the first site to prove that people lived here 11,000 years ago. The visitor center describes the site and its findings. You and your children can follow a paved walkway to an overhang for views of the treasures.

Oasis State Park (all ages)

Highway 467, 6 miles north of Portales just beyond Blackwater Draw Archaeological Site; (505) 356–5331. Admission: $5.00 for day use, $10.00 for overnight ($4.00 extra with hookup).

If you want to camp in this area, Oasis State Park offers 194 acres. There are nicely shaded, developed campsites and a fishing lake with catfish and trout.

Natural History Museum (all ages)

On the campus of Eastern New Mexico University on US 70; (505) 562–2174. **Open Monday through Friday 8:00 A.M. to 5:00 P.M. Admission: Free.**

The museum has both live and stuffed animals for the kids to see.

Where to Eat

El Rancho Restaurant. 101 South Chicago Avenue; (505) 359–0098. Mexican and American food. Open Monday through Friday 10:30 A.M. to 9:00 P.M., Saturday and Sunday 7:00 A.M. to 3:00 P.M. for a breakfast buffet. $–$$

Mark's Eastern Grill. 1126 West First Street; (505) 359–0857. Sandwiches, burgers, and a full children's menu. Open daily 7:00 A.M. to 9:00 P.M. $$

Wagon Wheel Cafe. 1001 West First Street; (505) 356–5036. Mexican and American food, plus a children's menu. Open Sunday through Thursday 6:00 A.M. to 8:00 P.M., Friday and Saturday to 9:00 P.M. $–$$

Where to Stay

Classic American Economy Inn. Highway 70 West; (505) 356–6668 or (800) 901–9466. $–$$

Morning Star Inn Bed and Breakfast. 620 West Second Street; (505) 356–2994. $$

Sands Motel. 1130 West First Street; (505) 356–4424. $

For More Information

Chamber of Commerce/Visitor Bureau. 200 East Seventh Street; (505) 356–8541 or (800) 635–8036; www.portales.com.

Clovis

At the junction of US 60 and US 70.

This area has a history similar to that of most of New Mexico: the mammoths, then the Indians, then the Spaniards, then the ranchers, then the railway. The daughter of one of the railway officials finally named it for Clovis, the king of the Franks, who converted to Christianity in the year 496. Now it is home to Cannon Air Force Base, numerous small ranches, and Clovis Community College.

Hillcrest Park and Zoo (all ages)

Junction of Sycamore and Tenth Streets; (505) 769–7873. **Open Tuesday through Sunday 9:00 A.M. to 5:00 P.M. Admission: $2.00 for adults, $1.00 for children 12 and under.**

The second-largest zoo in New Mexico. There are also a petting zoo for the kids, a swimming pool, and soccer fields.

Ned Houk Park and Pappy Thornton Homestead (all ages)

Highway 209, 6½ miles north of Clovis; (505) 769–7870. **Park and museum open Monday through Friday 7:00 A.M. to 3:00 P.M. Admission: Free.**

The park offers fishing, volleyball courts, and hiking trails, while the homestead has a museum with an excellent collection of old-time farm equipment that your children will find amazing in this age of computer games and supermarkets.

Golden **Oldies**

Check out **Norman Petty Recording Studios** on North Main Street (505–356–6422). It was the studio in which music greats like Buddy Holly, Waylon Jennings, and Roy Orbison recorded some of their hits. By appointment only.

Where to Stay

Clovis Inn. 2912 Mabry Drive; (505) 762–5600. Ninety-six rooms (some suites). Swimming pool. **Free** continental breakfast. No pets. $–$$

Comfort Inn. 1616 Mabry Drive; (505) 762–4591. Fifty rooms and a swimming pool make up this inn. $–$$

Holiday Inn. 2700 Mabry Drive; (505) 762–4491. The inn has 120 rooms, a swimming pool, a restaurant and lounge.

For More Information

Chamber of Commerce/Visitor Center.
215 North Main Street; (505) 763–3435;
www.clovisnm.org.

Annual **Community Events**

FIRST WEEKEND IN JUNE
Pioneer Days. Main Street and fairgrounds; (505) 763–3435. Includes a rodeo, a chile cook-off, pageants, and a wild cow milking (dare ya!).

FOURTH OF JULY
Smoke on the Water. Downtown; (505) 763–3435. Fireworks over the water and other events.

Southwest
New Mexico

A t first glance, this part of New Mexico seems too remote to be interesting. But although it's nearly all wilderness, if your family loves the outdoors, this is the region for you. There's still a lot of history here as well. The White Sands Missile Range and Trinity Site are near Socorro (see Alamogordo in previous chapter). La Mesilla, where Billy the Kid was tried for murder at the courthouse, is a part of the southwest region. Billy's family cabin is in Silver City, as is the Star Hotel, where New Mexico's most infamous citizen once waited on tables. At the more northerly end of this region, you and your family will delight in the Bosque del Apache Wildlife Refuge just outside Socorro.

Southwest New Mexico is also home to the 3½-million-acre Gila National Forest. Here the family can enjoy camping, hiking, and fishing as well as a look at the 600-year-old Gila Cliff Dwellings. A little bit to the east of Silver City is the Santa Rita Open Pit Copper Mine, the oldest copper mine in the state. You can also sample the best green chile in Hatch and cool off with a swim in Elephant Butte Lake, one of the largest man-made lakes in the world.

SOUTHWEST

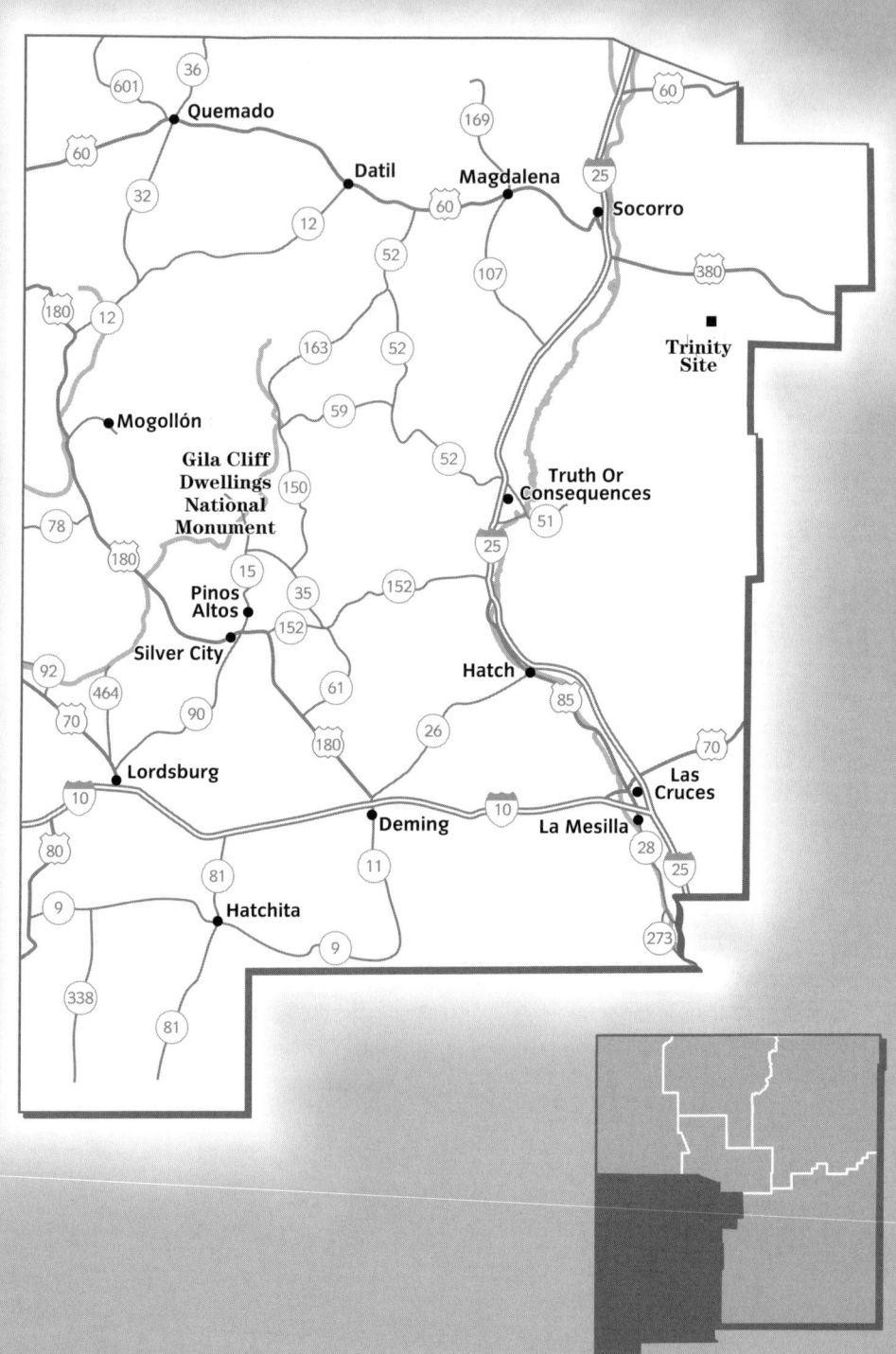

Quemado

U.S. Highway 60 west from Socorro.

This is another truly remote part of the country.

The Lightning Field (ages 10 to 12)
(505) 898–3335; thelightningfield@diacenter.org. Open daily May 1 to October 31. Admission: $110 per person in May, June, September, and October; $135 per person in July and August (advance registration required).

The best and really only reason to visit Quemado is to experience the Lightning Field. Land artist Walter de Maria decided to capitalize on the area's intense lightning storms when he created this piece in 1977, which was commissioned by the Dia Center for the Arts. He took 400 20-foot shiny metal rods, placed them in a carefully engineered grid and created an environmental art experience. The result is strange and beautiful. To experience the Lightning Field, you must make reservations with the Dia Center and plan to stay overnight. The center maintains a spare but comfortable cabin on the property, which sleeps six (if there are fewer than that in your party, you may be sharing the cabin with other visitors) and provides guests with a vegetarian dinner and breakfast foods. You meet a guide in the town of Quemado who will drive you out to the remote field and pick you up in the morning. Storms are most prevalent in July and August, but, really, there's no wrong time to visit this spectacular and important art site.

Quemado Lake (all ages)
US 60, then south on Highway 32. Open year-round. Free.

This man-made body of water resulted from the damming of Largo Creek. It's isolated, gorgeous, and full of the best fish in New Mexico. If you and your kids like to spend a happy afternoon with rod and reel and a big picnic, this is the place to take a break. There's no camping here, but it makes for a delightful afternoon in the sun with the family.

Datil

Junction of US 60 and Highway 12, about 45 miles west of Socorro.

This minuscule village was once a major rest stop for all cattle drives on their way to the Magdalena depot.

Datil Well (all ages)
On US 60.

This rugged campground would be a good place to set up camp to explore the tip of Catron County and the Gila National Forest. It's a beautiful spot, but basic. You have access to water but nothing else. Here the kids can enjoy the natural surroundings and get the feel of the frontier life of a cattle driver camping on the trail.

Where to Eat and Stay

Eagle Guest Ranch and Restaurant.
Intersection of Highway 12 and US 60, about 60 miles west of Socorro; (505) 772–5612. This charming, friendly motel and RV park (with hookups and a campground) welcomes families and is the only game in town. The restaurant serves that staple of the Western diet, chicken fried steak. The restaurant is open Monday through Saturday 6:00 A.M. to 9:00 P.M. $$

Socorro

Interstate–25 at US 60.

The unpretentious town of Socorro is an hour south of Albuquerque, directly off I–25. Its name is Spanish for "succor" or "caring help," reflecting the generosity of the local Indians during the Oñate expedition in 1598. Set in the lush Middle Rio Grande Valley, this town quickly became a rest stop or *paraje* for soldiers and supply caravans traveling the Camino Real—the Royal Road—between Mexico City and Santa Fe. Socorro has had a stop-and-start history, though: It was abandoned during the Pueblo Revolt in 1680 but was later resettled in 1816. It is a quiet, safe town where you will enjoy staying while you explore the delights of the region.

Old Plaza (all ages)
A walking tour of the Old Plaza (also known as Kittrel Park) is a good way to see the most attractive part of the town. First pick up the easy-to-follow map of Socorro at the Chamber of Commerce.

San Miguel Church (all ages)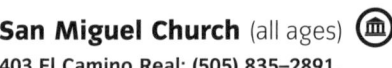
403 El Camino Real; (505) 835–2891.

Be sure to take the kids to see this pretty church directly behind the Old Plaza. It was built in 1821 over the ruins of a 1628 mission church. It has beautiful carved beams (called *vigas*), a bell tower, and 5-foot-thick walls (they weren't going to let *this* one be destroyed so easily).

Garcia Opera House (all ages)
110 Abeyta Avenue; (505) 835–9826.

Traveling opera companies performed for the frontier citizens who thought they needed culture. You and the kids can almost feel how exciting it must have been to hear all that grand music from the stage of this tiny, tilting, neo-Greek adobe opera house.

Mineralogical Museum (ages 10 to 12)
On the campus of the New Mexico Institute of Mining and Technology, off Olive Lane behind Workman Center; (505) 835–5420. Open Monday through Friday 8:00 A.M. to 5:00 P.M., Saturday and Sunday 10:00 A.M. to 3:00 P.M. Admission: Free.

The kids will enjoy the display of one of the most complete mineral collections in the world. Some of the minerals glow in the dark, and there are a lot of fossils to take a look at. The best part is the box of free rock specimens that the kids can pick through.

Bosque del Apache Wildlife Refuge (all ages)
I–25 south, off the San Antonio exit; (505) 835–1828. Open year-round from one hour before sunrise to one hour after sunset. Admission: $3.00.

This must be the focus of your visit to this area. This 1,500-acre site (*bosque* means "forest") is home to thousands of sandhill cranes, snow geese, whooping cranes, and egrets. There are also wild turkeys and white-tailed deer for the kids to enjoy. The best time to visit is in the late fall when all the birds fly in for the winter. The vast park has well-marked driving roads that take you and the family through the best parts of the refuge. Your kids will never forget the sight of thousands of snow geese looking like white blossoms dancing at the edge of the water. There are picnic tables around the visitor center but no restaurant. Every November the park hosts the Festival of the Cranes. For more information, see Annual Community Events in this section.

Water Canyon (all ages)
US 60, 13 miles west of Socorro; (505) 854–2281.

Part of the Cibola National Forest, this is another wildlife area great for seeing pronghorn antelope, golden eagles, and some of the birds from the Bosque that stop for a visit.

Owl Cafe and Steakhouse **in San Antonio**

After a day at the Bosque, you and the kids might want to stop for a slap-up wonderful hamburger dinner here. It's been in business since 1945, and the place is full of owls—stuffed and otherwise—that should keep the kids (and the owls) occupied until the food arrives. Open daily except Sunday from 8:30 A.M. to 9:00 P.M. First and Main Streets; (505) 835–9946. (This San Antonio is about 5 miles south of Socorro—not in Texas!)

Magdalena (all ages)
US 60, 27 miles west of Socorro; (866) 854–3217.

Before you leave the Socorro area, a fun place to take the kids is this old cowboy town named for Mary Magdalene. In 1884 the place was known as "trail's end" because cattle from ranches all over the Southwest were shipped out of the town's railroad depot. Today, it is an art town, with gift shops and a few pleasant cafes. The kids will get an eyeful of a real Wild West town.

La Joya Waterfowl Area (all ages)
I–25 north to US 60 east, then County Road 304 south for 7 miles; (505) 835–1828. Open year-round.

La Joya (pronounced La HOY-a) has 3,500 acres of wildlife and waterfowl. The refuge allows waterfowl hunting (call about permits). Again, bring plenty of water and picnic food.

Where to Eat

Frank and Lupe's El Sombrero. 210 Mesquite Street NE; (505) 835–3945. A reasonably priced and charming Mexican restaurant with water fountains and a fireplace. Children's menu. Open daily 11:00 A.M. to 9:00 P.M. $–$$

Val Verde Steakhouse. 203 Manzanares; (505) 835–3380; www.vvsteakh.com. Once upon a time this was a first-class railroad hotel. A wide selection of steak and seafood with a knock-out enchilada. Open Monday through Friday for lunch and dinner, Saturday and Sunday for dinner only. $–$$$

Very **Large Array (VLA)**

US 60, 50 miles west of Socorro, left on Highway 52; (505) 772–4011. Visitor center is open year-round from 8:30 A.M. to sunset. Guided tours are offered on weekends during the summer.

Be prepared to lay eyes on an amazing sight. Suddenly, white radar dishes begin appearing on the landscape bordering the road. This is really a twenty-seven-dish telescope spread out across the moonscape of the Plains of San Augustin. As you and your kids drive along the road, you almost feel as if you're on another planet, what with the barren landscape and these strange dishes. The kids will love it. The telescope is actually a listening device introduced in 1981 to pick up the faintest radio waves emitted by celestial objects. This is a segment of a four-region system that spreads across the country. A caution here: This is an extremely remote area, so bring everything with you that you think you will need, and wear sturdy, high boots if you decide to walk around—this is rattlesnake country.

Annual **Community Events**

LATE SEPTEMBER
San Miguel Fiesta. Old San Miguel Mission, 403 El Camino Real; (505) 835–2891. Music, dancing, and good food, followed by a processional mass on Sunday.

EARLY OCTOBER
Enchanted Skies Star Party. New Mexico Institute of Mining and Technology; (505) 835–0424. Amateur astronomers gather here from around the country to star-talk.

NOVEMBER
Festival of the Cranes at the Bosque del Apache. Highway 1, 8 miles south of San Antonio; (505) 835–0424 or (505) 835–1828. The refuge holds a four-day gathering of bird enthusiasts and specialists. There are tours, lectures, and opportunities to see parts of the refuge not usually open to the public. Families love the laid-back atmosphere of the event because kids have the run of the place and get to see eagles and hawks up close.

Where to Stay

Holiday Inn Express. 1100 California Avenue NE; (505) 838–0556. There are 120 rooms in this very nice, comfortable motel decorated in the Southwestern style. $–$$

Super 8 Motel. 1121 Frontage Road; (505) 835–4626. Eighty-eight rooms. Standard, well-kept motel. Restaurant nearby and laundry facilities on site. $

For More Information

Chamber of Commerce. 103 Francisco de Avondo; (505) 835–0424; www.socorronm.com.

Truth or Consequences

I–25 at Highway 51.

Like many other towns and small cities in this part of the state, Truth or Consequences has seen better days. Once it was a big, prosperous mining town called Hot Springs for its medicinal hot-spring wells. After the glory days of the gold and silver mines, Hot Springs settled into obscurity. When TV personality Ralph Edwards asked for a town in the United States to change its name to "Truth or Consequences" to commemorate the show's tenth anniversary, Hot Springs obliged. Thus the name. Most New Mexicans just call it "T or C."

Ralph Edwards Park (all ages)
Downtown Truth or Consequences.

Located along the Rio Grande, this park offers a wonderful place to break for a picnic lunch. There are sheltered tables, a playground, a horseshoe pit, a skateboard ramp, and restrooms.

Geronimo Springs Museum (all ages)
211 Main Street; (505) 894–6600. Open Monday through Saturday 9:00 A.M. to 5:00 P.M. Admission: $2.00 for adults, $1.00 for children 6–18.

This museum is full of unlabeled local history displays with some hands-on exhibits for the kids. It's built over the hot springs that the Apache chief Geronimo once used. The hot springs are still in operation, too, if you feel like treating the family to a good soak. There are indoor tubs and saunas, as well as the hot springs themselves.

Elephant Butte Lake State Park and Dam (all ages)
I–25 south at exit 83, then follow the signs on Highway 51 east; (505) 744–5421. Visitor center hours are 7:30 A.M. to 4:30 P.M. Admission: $65.00 for the day, $8.00–$10.00 for overnight ($4.00 extra with hookup).

A good reason to pass through Truth or Consequences is to get to this magnificent lake. This 40,000-acre body of water is New Mexico's largest lake, with 250 miles of shoreline

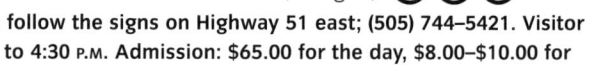

Ghost Towns **Chloride and Winston**

I–25 to Highway 52, 42 miles northwest of Truth or Consequences.

They aren't exactly ghost-ridden, because several of the old mining houses have been claimed and are being rebuilt, but the kids will enjoy seeing even the remnants of these mining ghost towns. Bring your own grub and stop for a rest and a picnic.

Annual **Community Events**

FIRST WEEKEND IN MAY
Truth or Consequences Fiesta. Downtown; (505) 894–3536. Also called the Ralph Edwards Fiesta, this event is known for its dances, a carnival, and different sporting and art events.

for you and the kids to enjoy; the largest shank of the lake extends 14 miles. It's a good idea to stop in at the visitor center just because the park is so big. There's tent and RV camping along with fishing, boating, cabins, a restaurant, fishing supplies, a food store, and a night fishing area. Your children will love being here; you may have to drag them away. Elephant Butte makes a vacation destination in itself!

Caballo Lake State Park (all ages)
I–25, 16 miles south of Truth or Consequences; (505) 743–3942. Admission: $5.00 for the day, $8.00–$10.00 for overnight ($4.00 extra with hookup).

This is another large body of water, covering some 11,000 acres. The lake is not as glamorous as Elephant Butte, but the kids can still enjoy swimming, boating, and fishing here. There are plenty of campsites, both primitive and with electricity and showers.

Percha Dam State Park (all ages)
I–25 exit 59 south on U.S. Highway 85 for 1 mile. Turn left on the dirt road at the sign; follow for 1.1 miles to the lake; (505) 743–3942.

The park is so close to Caballo Lake State Park that the State Parks Department runs them as one entity. Everything offered in Caballo is also offered here.

Where to Eat

Bar-B-Que on Broadway. 308 North Broadway; (505) 894–7047. Brisket, pork, turkey, and more smoked on the premises. Open Monday through Saturday 7:00 A.M. to 4:00 P.M. $–$$

La Cocina. 1 Lakeway Drive; (505) 894–6499. This is the local place for good and full plates of Mexican food (also burgers and sandwiches). Children's menu. Open 10:30 A.M. to 10:00 P.M. $–$$

Los Arcos Steakhouse. 1400 North Date Street; (505) 894–6200. Seafood and steak and an attractive hacienda-style decor. Salad bar and children's menu available. Open evenings only from 5:00 to 9:30 P.M. $–$$$

Where to Stay

Best Western Hot Spring Motor Inn.
2279 North Date Street; (505) 894–6665. The
inn has forty well-kept rooms. Children under
6 **free**. Heated outdoor pool. Complimentary cable television and coffee in the lobby.
$–$$

Rio Grande Motel. 720 Broadway, Williams-
burg (4 miles south of Truth or Consequences);
(505) 894–9769. Exit 75 off I–25. Attractive
place to stay close to Caballo Lake and Elephant Butte. Fifty rooms (some kitchenette-
style with refrigerators, hot plates, and
dishware) fill the motel. Playground, cable television, and laundry facilities are available, as
well as boat battery chargers! Small recreation area next door. $–$$

For More Information

Chamber of Commerce. (505) 894–3536
or (800) 831–9487; www.truthor
consequencesnm.net.

Silver City

I–25 south to the Caballo exit, then Highway 152 west for about 120 miles (no gas stations
between Caballo and Silver City) to Highway 90.

Silver City was recently voted one of the healthiest places to live in the country. No wonder. It's surrounded by 3½ million acres of stunning wilderness that draws visitors by the
thousands. Once you get to Silver City, you ll find it a small, old-fashioned town full of Victorian houses and offering a mild climate in all seasons. The Chamber of Commerce has
created some self-guided tours of the historical areas and buildings of both the city and
surrounding districts. There's an especially good one on Billy the Kid (tour #1b, "Billy's
Roots"). Billy and his family lived here; you can stop off at the sites of Billy's boyhood
home, his mother's grave, the restaurant where Billy waited tables, and the site of his first
escape from jail.

Silver City Museum (ages 10 to 12)

312 West Broadway; (505) 538–5921; www.silvercitymuseum.org. Open Tuesday through
Friday 9:00 A.M. to 4:30 P.M., Saturday and Sunday 10:00 A.M. to 4:00 P.M. Admission:
Free.

This is a big tourist draw, with its displays of frontier Victoriana and historical artifacts of
the area, as well as a wealth of old photos the kids will have fun matching up to the mod-

ern town. It shows you and the kids a lot of what life was like in a booming mining town in the 1880s. There's a gift shop, too.

Western New Mexico University Museum (all ages)
1000 West College Avenue; parking lot is near the museum located in Fleming Hall; (505) 538–6386. Open Monday through Friday 9:00 A.M. to 4:30 P.M., Saturday and Sunday 10:00 A.M. to 4:00 P.M. Gift shop. Admission: **Free.**

This is another big draw in the town, which the kids will thoroughly enjoy. There are displays of fossil mammoth tusks, ancient cutting tools, pottery, and arrow points from the nearby Mongollón Pueblo settlements. The building itself is an architectural gem.

Where to Eat

Adobe Springs Cafe. 1617 Silver Heights Boulevard; (505) 538–3665. Good varied menu. Open daily 7:00 A.M. to 9:00 P.M. $–$$

Buckhorn Saloon. Highway 15 in Pinos Altos; (505) 538–9911. Historic saloon with an Old West decor. Occasional live music. Steak, seafood specialties. Open Monday through Saturday 3:00 to 10:00 P.M. $$–$$$

Drifter Pancake House. 711 Silver Heights; (505) 538–2916. Attached to the Drifter Motel; serving breakfast items from 6:00 A.M. to 2:00 P.M. $–$$

Where to Stay

Copper Manor Motel. 710 Silver Heights Boulevard; (505) 538–5392. Sixty-eight comfortable rooms make up the motel. Restaurant and bar on premises and an indoor swimming pool. Children under 10 **free.** $

The Cottages. 2037 Cottage San Road; (505) 388–3000. These secluded 1930s cottages and suites feature wood burning stoves and feather beds. $$$

The Drifter Motel. 711 Silver Heights; (505) 538–2916 or (800) 853–2916. Sixty-nine rooms, some with refrigerators. Restaurant on site. $

Other Things **to Do**

- **Santa Rita Open Pit Copper Mine.** Highway 152, 25 miles east of Silver City; open on weekdays only. If you and your children have never seen open-pit mining, this is your chance. The Santa Rita is the oldest active mine in the Southwest and was once the largest open-pit copper mine in the world. Copper has come out of here since 1880, but the open-pit concept began in 1910. The kids will be riveted watching the gigantic machines eating into the mountainside and hauling off tons of dirt and ore in dump trucks the size of some people's houses.

- **Mogollón.** US 180 to Highway 159 east for 9 miles. This hamlet in Catron County is New Mexico's largest, most sparsely populated area. It's also in the Gila National Forest. You'll probably want to start early and leave early unless you are camping. Most people stay in Silver City, about 80 miles to the south. This once lawless gold, silver, and copper mining camp (not even the troops sent by the governor, nor the Apache chief Geronimo, could tame it) is now nearly a ghost town, but it's interesting for the kids to see. This is what Butch Cassidy and his Hole-in-the-Wall Gang called home. This place is really out of the way, but it's a good example of a life long gone.

- **Whitewater Creek and Catwalk.** US 180 and Highway 174 to Glenwood (just beyond Mogollón). Fun! The kids will be thrilled, especially if you visit late in spring, when the snows melt from the San Francisco Mountains that rim the valley. The water gushes down, filling Whitewater Creek to bursting, and funnels through a gorge of rocks 100 feet deep, roaring its way downhill. What the kids will love is the catwalk, a steel walkway that hangs over the creek. You can follow the flow of the river while hanging some 20 feet over it. The trail follows the water up and down, sometimes nearly in it, and walkers get to cross over some interesting bridges. To be this close to a roaring flow of water is an experience the children shouldn't miss. Bring a picnic lunch, because it's a great place to lie back and enjoy the scenery and listen to the creek whirl by. The area is wide open and easily accessible.

Annual Community Events

FOURTH OF JULY WEEKEND
Independence Day Celebration. Gough Park; (505) 538–3785 or (800)
548–9378. Begins with breakfast in the park at 7:30 A.M. and a parade at
10:00 A.M. An ice-cream social at the Silver City Museum with music, dancing,
and other entertainment follows.

For More Information

Chamber of Commerce. 201 North
Hudson Avenue; (505) 538–3785 or (800)
548–9378; www.silvercity.org.

Pinos Altos

Highway 90 north to Highway 15 north, 7 miles from Silver City.

"Tall Pines" is a great little dirt-road village that began as a mining town under Apache (and
sometimes Navajo) siege in 1868. The famous Judge Roy Bean had a general store in town.

Buckhorn Saloon (ages 10 to 12) 🏛️ 🍴
Highway 15 in center of Pinos Altos, 7 miles north of Silver City; (505) 538–9911.
This is a unique experience for the kids. They'll get a kick out of its genuine Wild West
atmosphere. The saloon actually serves food, so you can stop and get a bite. Have your
kids keep an eye out for Indian Joe, who sits at the bar and welcomes the tourists. Ask
about the ghost stories!

For Further Reference

Geronimo: His Own Story by Geronimo, Stephen Melvil Barrett, and others
(Plume Books). First published in 1906, this is the autobiography of the
Apache chief who was legendary in this area for his ferocious resistance to
the efforts of the U.S. government to relocate his people.

Gila National Forest, Cliff Dwellings, and Hot Springs

Gila National Forest (all ages)

From Silver City: Highway 90 north to Highway 15 north; (505) 388–8201.

The Gila National Forest dominates the southwestern part of the state. There are opportunities for you and your family to enjoy camping, hiking, fishing, even snowmobiling in the Gila. There are 1,510 miles of hiking trails and eighteen campgrounds (both primitive and developed), with 790,000 acres set aside as deep wilderness. While hiking these areas, you and the kids should keep an eye out for black bear, mountain lions, and bighorn sheep that roam the forest. There are two lakes that are also part of the park, SNOW LAKE (off the dirt-road portion of Highway 159) and WALL LAKE (28 miles south of the dirt-road portion of Highway 159). Both offer fishing, camping, and hiking for the family. Be careful; you are likely to enter some extremely remote areas while here. Go prepared with enough food, water, and Gameboy batteries, with a full tank of gas.

Gila Cliff Dwellings National Monument (all ages)

Highway 15 north, 40 miles from Pinos Altos; (505) 536–9344; www.nps.gov/gicl. Open daily from 8:00 A.M. to 6:00 P.M.

Your children will be enthralled by these ancient homes. The monument preserves the cliff dwellings of the Mogollón Pueblo Indians who inhabited these rock houses from 1280 to 1380. The area is remote and rugged, so wear sturdy hiking shoes and clothing, and bring plenty of high-energy snacks and water. It's a hefty hike of about a mile to get to the cliffs, then you need to climb another 200 to 300 feet to the dwellings themselves (you may wonder how anyone found them at all as you walk). It is a moving experience, in more ways than one, for the whole family. The kids will be able to explore these remarkable adobe and timber houses and almost feel the presence of this ancient tribe.

Gila Hot Springs (all ages)

The visitor center is located 2 miles from the monument entrance; (505) 536–9551. Open daily from sunrise to sunset.

There are three springs accessed via routes of varying degrees of difficulty. The easiest is located near Doc Campbell's Post, on your way to the visitor center (and the only store for miles, by the way, if you've run out of anything). It is 4 miles below the Gila Cliff Dwellings. There are privately owned campgrounds here, as well as an RV park. Check with the visitor center for details on the other campsites located deeper in the forest.

Valverde **Battlefield**

I–25, south of Socorro

This was the site of the first Civil War battle fought on New Mexico soil. In February 1862 General H. H. Sibley's Confederate forces defeated Colonel E. R. S. Canby's Union forces stationed at Fort Craig. The fort is now under the waters of Elephant Butte Lake. Sibley (who had defected from his Union duties earlier at Fort Union) was later defeated at the battle of Glorieta Pass in March of the same year.

Deming

US 70/Interstate 10 at US 180.

This is another small town that serves as a major rest stop along I–10. It was founded in 1881 when the Santa Fe and Southern Pacific Railroads were linked, thus creating the first direct route from the Atlantic to the Pacific coast.

Deming Luna Mimbres Museum (all ages)

National Guard Armory, 301 South Silver Avenue; (505) 546–2382. Open Monday through Saturday from 9:00 A.M. to 4:00 P.M., Sunday from 1:30 to 4:00 P.M. Admission: Free

The museum is a good stop for the kids. It has cowboy artifacts, including chuck wagons and cowboy clothes, guns, memorabilia from Deming's World War II veterans, and a few dinosaur goodies. There's also a huge doll and toy room representing most wish lists from 1850 until the present time.

Pancho Villa State Park and Fort Furlong (all ages)

In Columbus, 30 miles south of Deming along Highway 11; (505) 531–2711. Admission: $5.00 for the day, $10.00 for overnight ($4.00 extra with hookup).

This is a major attraction in the region, and a great history lesson for your kids, because it is here that the great Mexican bandito Pancho Villa launched an attack on the continental United States. Villa stole into Camp Furlong at dawn on a cold March morning in 1916. He tried to surprise the U.S. Army forces stationed there, after reputedly having tried to ambush a train full of gold. But he had to deal with General John Pershing, who would go on to win fame in World War I. Needless to say, Pancho Villa failed, but he lives on in history, and this park commemorates his foolhardy foray. Pershing followed Villa into Mexico. He never did find Villa, however, who continued as a bandit until 1920, when he retired (he was assassinated in 1923). Some think that there is still a stash of Pancho Villa's loot in the Providence Cone west of Las Cruces. What you see now at the fort are mostly ruins,

Faywood **Hot Springs**

165 Highway 61, 2 miles after it intersects with US 180, next to City of Rocks State Park; (505) 536–9663; www.faywood.com. Open daily 10:00 A.M. to 10:00 P.M. Public pools are $10 per person.

Enjoy geothermal pools for the whole family. Some of the pools are private (you can wear a bathing suit, or not), and some are public. Stay in the cedar and oak cabins that have kitchenettes and baths (the tub kind), or in a 16-foot teepee. You can get a massage, too.

but there are markers about what happened where. In addition to all this history, there are more than sixty campsites for you and your family to use as you rest up for your trip back.

City of Rocks State Park (all ages)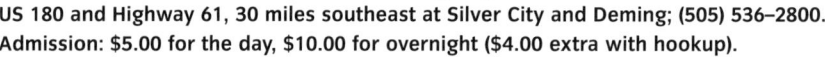

US 180 and Highway 61, 30 miles southeast at Silver City and Deming; (505) 536–2800. Admission: $5.00 for the day, $10.00 for overnight ($4.00 extra with hookup).

This is a memorable place and well worth the time taken for such a side trip. You and your family will come upon this odd and remarkable collection of upright boulders and think you're seeing some kind of Druid worship site. Actually, it's "welded tuff," the leftover product of the huge volcanic eruptions of thirty million years ago. Over the centuries the rock eroded to form these fantastical shapes. Kids love this place. They can run around through the arches and over the gigantic formations and imagine a Fred Flintstone world. What makes it more fun is that the family can picnic and camp here, too (sites are dotted throughout, and there are water and shower facilities). There's even a playground.

Ghost Towns of **Shakespeare and Steins**

In Lordsburg on I–10, exit 3. Shakespeare is about an hour west of Deming; Steins is 1½ hours from Deming; (505) 542–9034 for Shakespeare; (505) 542–9791 for Steins.

Shakespeare is listed on the National Register of Historic Places. It started as a mining swindle in the 1870s, then grew legitimately during the 1908–1932 mining boom. This town had no social restraints: no church, no newspaper, no law enforcement. Guided tours are available, and four times a year there are reenactments of a "typical" day in Shakespeare. Steins (pronounced "steens") was established in 1858 as a railroad town, serving the Butterfield Line. Now it has ten buildings left full of artifacts (including a rattlesnake exhibit). There are tours available as well as picnic supplies.

Where to Eat

El Camino Real. 900 West Pine Street; (505) 546–7421. Mexican and American fare, seafood, and a children's menu. Open daily 7:00 A.M. to 8:00 P.M. $

La Fonda Restaurant. 601 East Pine Street; (505) 546–0465. Excellent fajitas and other Mexican and American food. Open daily 6:00 A.M. to 8:00 P.M. $–$$

Rancher's Grill. 316 East Cedar; (505) 546–8883. Good steak, chicken, and seafood. Children's menu. Open daily 10:30 A.M. to 10:00 P.M. $$–$$$

Where to Stay

Grand Motor Inn. 1721 East Pine Street; (505) 546–2632. The inn has sixty standard, comfortable rooms. Swimming pool. Restaurant on site. $–$$

Holiday Inn. I–10 at exit 85; (505) 546–2661. 120 large rooms. Outdoor swimming pool. On-site laundry facilities and restaurant. $–$$

Wagon Wheel Motel. 1109 West Pine Street; (505) 546–2681. Here are nineteen rooms in a convenient setting. Small outdoor pool, laundry facilities. Restaurant nearby. Small pets welcome. $

For More Information

Chamber of Commerce. (505) 546–2674 or (800) 848–4955; www.demingchamber.com.

Annual Community Events

AUGUST
Great American Duck Races. State Fairgrounds; (888) 345–1125; www .demingduckrace.com. The world's greatest (and richest) duck races, with music and dancing, hot-air balloon races, and games, including a tortilla toss.

LATE SEPTEMBER–EARLY OCTOBER
Southwestern New Mexico State Fair. State Fairgrounds; (505) 546–2674 or (505) 546–3700. Rodeo, carnival, livestock and horticultural exhibits and contests, and lots of cotton candy.

Las Cruces

I–25 south to the Las Cruces exit (I–10).

"The Crosses" supposedly got its name from the crosses that marked the graves of forty Spanish settlers massacred by Apache on their way from Taos. It's also at a crossroads for those on the Camino Real, the Butterfield cattle trail, the railroad, and several main passenger highways. However the name came to be, Las Cruces is a pleasant town that is now the home of New Mexico State University. It's also a growing writers' and artists' colony.

Bicentennial Log Cabin (all ages)

671 North Main Street, at the north end of Downtown Mall; (505) 541–2155. Open only in the summer; tours by appointment.

The kids can see what one of these old-time pioneer cabins looked like on the inside. The little house is furnished as it would have been in the 1880s.

Las Cruces Museum of Natural History (all ages)

Mesilla Valley Mall, 700 Telshor Boulevard; (505) 522–3120. Open Monday through Thursday and Saturday 10:00 A.M. to 5:00 P.M., Friday to 8:00 P.M., and Sunday 1:00 to 5:00 P.M. Admission: Free.

This place is good for learning more about the natural science and history of southwestern New Mexico. There are field trips, family nights, and a children's newspaper.

New Mexico Farm and Ranch Heritage Museum (all ages)

4100 Dripping Springs Road (University Avenue East, 1½ miles past I–25); (505) 522–4100. Open Monday through Saturday 9:00 A.M. to 5:00 P.M., Sunday noon to 5:00 P.M. Admission: $3.00 for adults, $1.00 for children 6–17, children under 6 free.

This working farm offers guided tours covering more than 3,000 years of agricultural history. There is a gallery, indoor and outdoor theaters, and a restaurant that features homegrown vegetables. The Purple Sage Restaurant (505–532–1765) is open for lunch Tuesday through Sunday. Make a day of it.

Community **Swimming Pools**

- **Apodaca Pools:** 801 East Madrid; (505) 524–7008

- **Frenger Pool:** 800 Parkview Drive; (505) 523–0362

- **Laabs Pool:** 750 West Picacho Avenue; (505) 524–3168

Other Things **to Do**

La Mesilla. Highway 28, 1½ miles southwest of Las Cruces. This is a great little town that offers a little more Billy the Kid history. It's also a pretty Hispanic village that is a delight to stroll through. The kids will get to see the courthouse where Billy was tried for murder and jailed—until he escaped. The town also has historical significance as the site of the signing of the Gadsden Purchase in 1854. It was with this agreement that the international borders separating Mexico from New Mexico and Arizona were established. There are lots of cafes, coffee shops, and restaurants where you can stop for a break.

Fort Selden State Monument (ages 10 to 12)
I–25 north to exit 19 (Radium Springs) to Highway 185 west, 16 miles northwest of Las Cruces; (505) 526–8911. Open Wednesday through Monday 8:00 A.M. to 5:00 P.M. Admission: $3.00 for adults, children under 16 **free.**

Mostly in ruins, Fort Selden once had a glorious career protecting settlers from Apache raids. In later years it housed the famous Buffalo Soldiers, a U.S. Army Cavalry unit made up entirely of black soldiers. General Douglas MacArthur spent some of his childhood here. Kids can walk through the ruins and learn about the Buffalo Soldiers at the visitor center.

Aquirre Springs Recreation Site (all ages)
US 70 east; (505) 525–4300.

Run by the Bureau of Land Management, this area offers you and your children picnicking sites and trails for hiking and horseback riding.

Where to Eat

La Posta de Mesilla. 2410 Calle de San Albino, Mesilla; (505) 524–3524. Classic New Mexican food served in the historic La Posta Compound. Full children's menu. Open Tuesday through Thursday 11:00 A.M. to 9:00 P.M., Friday and Saturday to 9:30 P.M. $–$$

Tegmeyer's Salad Works. 1300 El Paseo; (505) 525–2323. Buffet items and discounted children's prices. Open daily 11:00 A.M. to 8:30 P.M. $

Camino **Real**

The "Royal Road" once spanned the 2,000 miles from Mexico City to Santa Fe. It was made "official" by Don Juan Oñate in 1598, when he marched on it as the first governor of what was then known as New Spain. Many of the towns existing now in this area began their life along the road when Oñate and his troops (and their families) established parajes, or campsites, along the way (he made these official, too).

Where to Stay

La Quinta Inn. 790 Avenida de Mesilla; (505) 524–0331. 139 Spanish-style rooms. Coffeemakers and cable television in all rooms; some rooms with refrigerators and whirlpools. Small pets welcome. $–$$

Las Cruces Hilton Inn. 705 South Telshor Boulevard; (505) 522–4300. 203 elegant Southwestern-style rooms. Centrally located with restaurant, heated outdoor pool, exercise room, and gift shop. Pets welcome in pool-level smoking rooms for an additional $20 fee. $$–$$$

Lundeen Inn of the Arts. 618 South Alameda Boulevard; (505) 526–3326; www.innofthearts.com. Built in 1890, the inn is part art gallery, part hotel. Each of the twenty rooms (including seven suites) is decorated and named after an artist. Complimentary continental breakfast and cable television. Exercise room and a recreational "lawn" for picnic games. Small pets welcome. $$–$$$

Annual **Community Events**

LABOR DAY WEEKEND
Hatch Chile Festival. Highway 26, at Hatch's airport, 30 miles north of Las Cruces; (505) 267–5050; www.villageofhatch.org. If your stay in New Mexico has gotten you hooked on chile peppers, then Hatch is an important stop. Considered the chile capital of the state, this is where they grow the best of the best. This harvest festival is fun, with carnival rides for the kids, cookoffs, and music galore. The smell of roasted chiles is wonderful.

LATE SEPTEMBER
Whole Enchilada Fiesta. Downtown Las Cruces; (505) 541–2444. The world's largest enchilada gets eaten (and enjoyed!). There are also a parade, music and dancing, and various exhibits.

For More Information

Chamber of Commerce. (505) 524–1968;
www.lascruces.org.

Visitors Bureau. 211 North Water Street;
(505) 541–2444; www.lascrucescvb.org.

Northwest
New Mexico

This is a remarkable corner of New Mexico where some of the state's most beautifully rugged scenery frames the heart of Native American culture. Navajo, Zuñi, Acoma, and Laguna nations live side by side among the pristine mesas and plains of northwest New Mexico.

The Northwest's major towns are Gallup, Farmington, and Grants, all of which are treasure troves chronicling the Western heritage. The famous Four Corners National Monument, near Farmington, is where Utah, Arizona, Colorado, and New Mexico meet. This entire area abounds in unforgettable sites for your family to experience. There are historic mines, Chaco Canyon, Indian pueblos, the magnificent Shiprock Peak edging the Navajo reservation, national and state parks, even a slice of the famous Route 66. While it will be fun exploring the different towns and the Native American cultures, the real life of northwestern New Mexico revolves around the magnificent landscape that envelops the area.

Farmington

U.S. Highway 64 and U.S. Highway 666.

This is an exciting area of the state because it includes spectacular natural wonders and a large chunk of the Navajo reservation. The largest reservation in the United States, it covers an area spreading over parts of Arizona, New Mexico, and Utah and equals in area the state of West Virginia. Three large rivers flow around Farmington, La Plata (The Silver), San Juan (Saint John), and the Animas (Spirits). This is a great place to catch a fish. Now a center for the gas and oil industry, Farmington was once a major trading center and part of the Jicarilla Apache reservation.

NORTHWEST

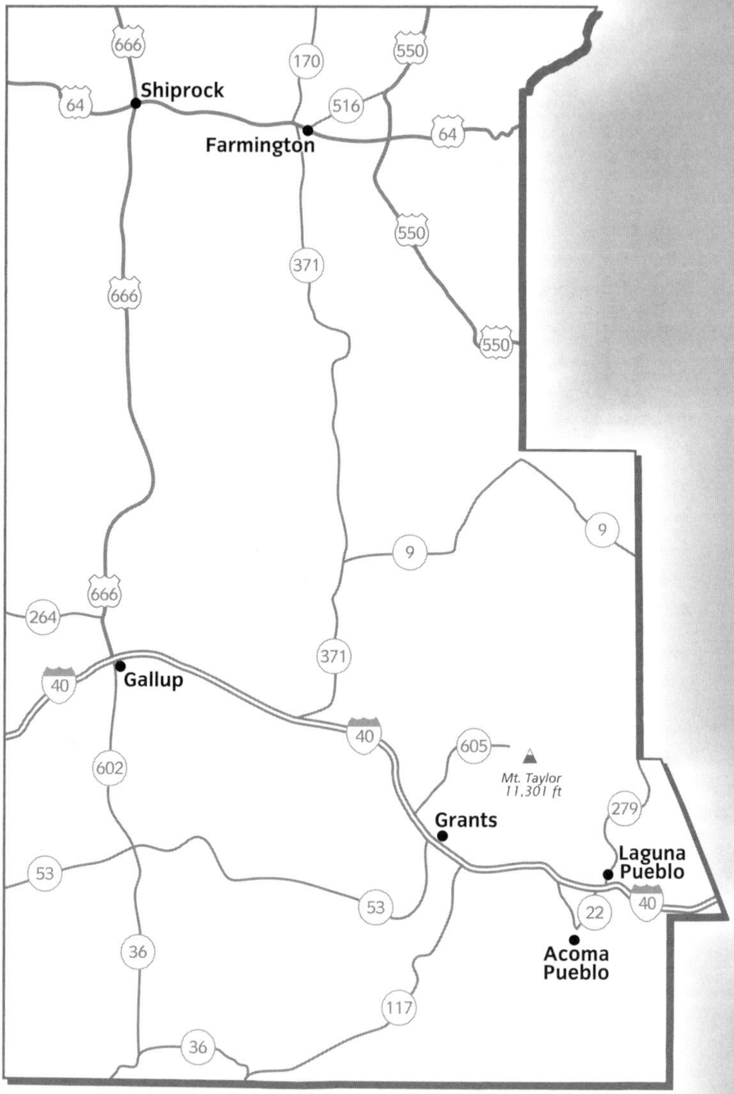

666

170

550

64 · **Shiprock**

516

Farmington · 64

550

371

550

666

9

9

264 · 666

371

40 · **Gallup**

40

602

605 ▲ *Mt. Taylor 11,301 ft*

Grants · 279

53 · **Laguna Pueblo** · 40

53

22

36 · **Acoma Pueblo**

117

36

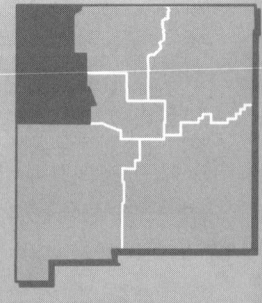

The Farmington Museum and E3 Children's Museum and Science Center (all ages)

Farmington Museum: 3041 East Main Street; (505) 599–1174. Open Monday through Saturday 8:00 A.M. to 5:00 P.M. Admission: Free. Children's Museum: 302 North Orchard Street; (505) 599–1425. Open Wednesday through Friday noon to 5:00 P.M., Saturday 10:00 A.M. to 5:00 P.M. Admission: Free.

The Farmington Museum can help orient you to some of the fascinating sights of the Four Corners area. The museum features a variety of changing exhibits and a few permanent ones, including a walk-through replica of a 1930s trading post. The E3 Children's Museum, an adjunct facility of the Farmington Museum, features interactive, hands-on, science-themed exhibits. Tot's Turf is a special room designed to engage children under six. **The Riverside Nature Center** (505–599–1422) and **Harvest Grove Farm and Orchards** (505–599–1174) are two other components of the Farmington Museum.

Lions Wilderness Park (all ages)

Out of Farmington: Take Thirtieth Street to College Boulevard North and follow it for 2 miles. (505) 327–9336 (information and schedule) or (877) 599–3331 (tickets). Performances are from mid-June to mid-August. Admission: $11.00 for adults, $9.00 for students and seniors, $6.00 for children 12 and under. Meal tickets for a Mexican buffet-style dinner are $8.00 to $9.00.

The outdoor amphitheater is in an area of high desert plateau with sandstone cliffs as a backdrop. Every summer, Sandstone Productions puts on shows like Black River Traders, about life in an early twentieth-century trading post, and Anasazi, The Ancient Ones, a musical drama full of songs and ceremonial dances about Native Americans and Anglo pioneers.

Animas Parkland and Berg Park (all ages)

Downtown Farmington along the Animas River at Scott Avenue and Highway 64 (Broadway).

For wildlife watching with some nature walking thrown in, this sixty-two-acre park offers 5 miles of riverside tracks along the Animas River.

Jackson Lake State Waterfowl Area (all ages)

Along the La Plata River, 5 miles north off La Plata Highway and Highway 64.

The park's 840 acres offer more nature paths and wildlife viewing, including ducks floating in the river and lake. Fishing and picnicking are available.

Salmon Ruin Heritage Park (all ages)

12 miles east of Farmington along Highway 64; (505) 632–2013. Open daily 9:00 A.M. to 5:00 P.M., Sunday noon to 5:00 P.M. November through March. Admission: $3.00 for adults, $2.00 for seniors, $1.00 for kids 6–16.

Many outdoor sights in this territory are at the end of some very rugged dirt roads, but the Salmon Ruins are easily accessed. Here you and your family can visit the remnants of an eleventh-century pueblo village (curiously, it was abandoned three times in sixty years) and the remains of the pioneer homestead of George Salmon. The park's Heritage Center is a marvelous experience for the children to enjoy some hands-on activities, such as weaving a Navajo rug (taught by a Navajo weaver), learning animal footprint identification, and actually making a petroglyph of their own.

Chaco Culture National Historical Park (all ages)

There are three routes into the park, all of which contain several-mile stretches of dirt road, which can become impassable in inclement weather. Call ahead for current road conditions. The best and easiest route is from the north, via U.S. Highway 550. Turn off at County Road 7900, 3 miles southeast of Nageezi; this route includes 5 miles of paved road and 16 miles of unpaved road. (505) 786–7014 or (800) 448–1240; www.nps.gov/chcu. Open daily at 8:00 A.M. Admission: $4.00 per person, $8.00 per vehicle. Tent camping $10 per night. There are forty-seven primitive sites available at the Gallo Campground (approximately 1 mile east of the visitor center) on a first come, first serve basis. Each has a picnic area and a fire grate (bring your own wood or charcoal; gathering firewood in the area is prohibited). There are restrooms, but no showers. The only potable water is at the visitor center. Free day-long backcountry hiking permits are also available.

Chaco Canyon is in the middle of nowhere, but it's one of the premier attractions in the state. You should know that there is no food, firewood, or gasoline here, and only camping and RV hookups for lodging, so bring everything that you will need with you. Plan to spend a few days; there is so much to see and do here. This is a rugged and truly remote area where ancient pueblo ruins date from A.D. 900. Familiarize yourselves with the area by taking advantage of the displays and information at the visitor center. The center shows a film about the Anasazi—Navajo "ancient ones—and offers maps of the areas open to the public. There are also scheduled walking tours available.

Nearly 1,000 years ago, close to 10,000 Anasazi are believed to have populated Chaco Canyon. If this is true, it was one of the biggest cities of the time in North America. They farmed and gathered roots and berries to sustain themselves and built some of the earliest pueblo living quarters. The grandest one of these is **Pueblo Bonito.** It contained 600 rooms, numerous kivas, and stood four stories high. The pueblo was built to serve as an astronomical observatory as well as housing. The Anasazi believed that this area was the center of the world and had great secrets to tell. The study of astronomy continues at modern-day Chaco Canyon: The park includes a well-equipped, state-of-the-art observatory where rangers host regular star watches and talks. Because the area is so remote, there is very little light pollution to inhibit astronomers' night viewing. Other sites to investigate are Chetro Ketl, Casa Rinconada, Pueblo Arroyo, and Casa Chiquita. You can take your kids

Doing **Time**

Yipes! The Federal Antiquities Act weighs in with a $100,000 fine and twenty-five years in Uncle Sam's prison if someone takes potsherds (broken pottery pieces) or any artifact from a place such as Chaco Canyon.

for a major hike in **Peñasco Blanco** where rock paintings of the sun and moon attest to the sacredness of this location. Park rangers are here to answer your questions. This is a wonderful place for kids to gain insights into the greatness of an ancient civilization.

Angel Peak Recreation Area (all ages)
20 miles south of Bloomfield on Highway 44 (the last 6 miles of it is gravel); (505) 599–8900. Six primitive campsites. Admission: Free

This is truly a remarkable place where you and your family can picnic or camp. As you drive to the edge of the recreation area, stop at either the Sage picnic site or the Angel Peak overlook. In the distance, Angel Peak itself commands the view. To the Navajos, Angel Peak is known as the Sacred Ones' Dwelling Place. As you look across this extraordinary landscape, you'll be able to see the San Juan Mountains, the La Plata dip, Shiprock, and the El Huérfano (the Orphan) mesa. This whole area, also called the Badlands, was an inland sea some forty million years ago, and you can still get that feeling if you examine the striated rock forms carefully. Just so you know, neither the campsites nor the picnic areas have running water, and only a few have shelters (pit toilets available).

Four Corners Monument (ages 10 to 12)
30 miles northwest of Shiprock off US 64 and U.S. Highway 160. Admission: $3.00 per person.

Stand on a surveyor's mark under a wooden roof in the middle of a barren spot, and you'll actually be in New Mexico, Arizona, Utah, and Colorado simultaneously. The monument is a stone slab that designates the only spot in the United States where you'll be able to stand in four states at once. There's not much else going on here, but it can be a fun experience for the kids. The edges surrounding the Four Corners mark have booths selling Indian jewelry and dream-catcher ornaments. There are also a couple of small caravans where the kids can snack on fry bread and sandwiches, and there are portable toilets in the parking lot.

Shiprock Pinnacle (ages 10 to 12)
US 64 and US 666, about an hour's drive from Farmington.

Watch for the 1,700-foot peak called by the Navajo the "Rock with Wings." You can only see it from a distance because it is considered a sacred site and not for visitors. But the best way to see this rock is from a distance. The sun plays across its expanse, and it shimmers in the heat and clouds of the desert that surrounds it. Sometimes it looks like a great ship, sometimes as though it could take flight.

Bisti/De-Na-Zin Wilderness (ages 10 to 12)
38 miles south of Bloomfield. From Farmington: Take US 64 East to Bloomfield (20 miles). Take U.S. Highway 44 South for 30 miles to the Huérfano Trading Post. Here, take CR 7500 (gravel) another 2 miles to the parking lot. For maps and the latest information, contact the Bureau of Land Management: (505) 599–8900.

This is one of the least visited spots in the state, but it is an exceptional experience. The 23,000-acre prehistoric wilderness has fossilized dinosaurs, plants, and reptiles for the kids to discover. Archaeologists believe it was once a dinosaur-infested swamp. Its name is Navajo for "tall or standing crane"—legend has it that the birds stopped to rest here on their way south for the winter. Be sure to take the children to see the Logjam, a 350-acre site of petrified logs 75 feet long and 6 feet around. *Be warned:* This is another area that comes under the Federal Antiquities Act. Taking stones, fossils, or petrified wood out of here is a federal offense. The area is patrolled. The De-Na-Zin is extremely remote, so bring plenty of food and water, sensible clothing, and shoes. Make sure that your car is in good repair. The campsites are rudimentary with no firewood supplies—or anything else.

Aztec Museum and Pioneer Village (ages 10 to 12)
Town of Aztec is 15 minutes from Farmington at Highway 544 and US 550. The museum is at 125 North Main Street; (505) 334–9829; www.aztecnm.com/museum/museum_main.htm. Open Monday through Saturday 9:00 A.M. to 5:00 P.M. Admission: $3.00 for adults, $1.00 for kids 11 and over.

More than half of Aztec's buildings are listed on the National Register of Historic Places. Take the Historic Aztec Walking Tour (pick up the guide at the visitor bureau) that includes those buildings and those on the New Mexico State Register. The town's name comes from a mispronunciation of the word "Anasazi" and was founded in 1876 when some of the Jicarilla Apache reservation was opened up for non-Indian settlement. The twelfth-century Pueblo ruins that are also a part of the historic district are well preserved, feature a walking trail, and contain the largest reconstructed kiva. Much of the ruins has yet to be excavated. The museum has a good collection of pioneer artifacts and prehistoric samples of local cultures. There is a pioneer village with a sheriff's office, a doctor's office, and a log cabin. There's also a gunfight at noon every day during the summer (except Sunday). The kids might find an oil field exhibit with a wooden oil drilling rig interesting, too.

Navajo Lake State Park (all ages)
23 miles east of Aztec along Highway 173 and 511; (505) 632–2278 or (505) 632–8734. Admission: $5.00 for the day, $10.00 for overnight stays (with $4.00 hookup charge).

There are three recreation areas in the park: Sims Mesa (across the lake via Highway 527), San Juan River (wheelchair accessible and renowned for the trout fishing), and Pine River (the most developed of the sites and site of the visitor center). They all overlook Navajo

Interesting **Arti-fact**

The artifacts that were found at the Aztec ruins show that the Anasazi were either skilled traders or they knew where the mall was. Among the items uncovered are jewelry from California seashells, bronze bells and parrot feathers from Mexico, and turquoise from Utah.

Lake, the largest in northwestern New Mexico. The lake is great for trout and bass fishing. The park has campsites, a visitor center, and three full-service marinas. Call first to find out what the conditions are (if the fish aren't biting, they'll tell you).

Where to Eat

Clancy's Pub and Restaurant. 2703 East Twentieth Street; (505) 325–8176. Good salads, sandwiches, and burgers. Open daily 11:00 A.M. to 11:00 P.M. $–$$

La Fiesta Grande. 1916 East Maine; (505) 326–6476. Very reasonably priced Mexican food. Open daily 11:00 A.M. to 9:00 P.M. $–$$

Sonya's Cookin USA. 2001 Bloomfield Highway; (505) 327–3526. The local breakfast (and lunch and dinner) habit. Good food in a casual setting. Open Monday through Saturday 6:00 A.M. to 8:30 P.M., Sunday 7:00 A.M. to 2:00 P.M. $–$$

Where to Stay

Best Western Inn and Suites. 700 Scott Avenue; (505) 327–5221 or (800) 528–1234.

Some of the 192 rooms have pull-out sleeper sofas and in-room bar. Indoor recreation center, restaurant, and laundry facilities. Small pets welcome. $$–$$$

Holiday Inn. 600 East Broadway; (505) 327–9811 or (800) HOLIDAY. The inn offers 150 units and a swimming pool. Restaurant on premises. $$

Travelodge Farmington. 510 Scott Avenue; (505) 327–0242. $$

For More Information

Chamber of Commerce. 105 North Orchard Avenue; (505) 325–0279; www.gofarmington.com.

Visitors Bureau. 3041 East Main Street; (505) 326–7602 or (800) 448–1240; www.farmingtonnm.org.

Annual **Community Events**

MEMORIAL DAY WEEKEND
Farmington International Balloon Festival. Farmington Lake; (800) 448–1240. Hot-air balloon launches; races at 6:00 A.M. Saturday and Sunday. Riverfest. (800) 448–1240. A celebration of the area's rivers, with music, entertainment, trail walks, and raft rides.

FOURTH OF JULY WEEKEND
Farmington Freedom Days. Downtown area; (800) 448–1240.
Auction, food fair, street dancing, parades, concerts, and fireworks.

AUGUST
Connie Mack World Series Baseball Tournament. Rickett's Park; (505) 327–9673. A week of baseball featuring top amateur players and pro scouts from the United States and Puerto Rico.

San Juan County Fair. McGee Park on US 64; (505) 325–5385 or (800) 448–1240. The largest county fair in New Mexico. Weeklong event features live concerts, a fiddling contest, parades, a carnival, and livestock shows.

LABOR DAY WEEKEND
Totah (Navajo for "Among the Rivers") Festival. Farmington Civic Center; (800) 448–1240. A Native American juried fine arts and crafts show and marketplace, including a rug auction and powwow.

EARLY OCTOBER
Annual Northern Navajo Nation Celebration.
Shiprock Fairgrounds; (800) 448–1240. Arts and crafts, a parade, rodeo, powwow, etc.

DECEMBER
Festival de los Farolitos and Parade of Lights.
(800) 448–1240. Beautiful display of traditional Spanish lanterns; Aztec ruins at dusk.

Gallup

I–40 at US 666 and Highway 602.

Gallup is the heart of Indian country. Founded in 1881, this unassuming city was named not for a horse's gait but for the paymaster of the Atlantic and Pacific Railroad, David L. Gallup. He had settled in this far corner of McKinley County and if the men wanted their pay packets, they had to "go to Gallup."

After coal mining began in the area, the town soon became a crossroads for cowboys, ranchers, and miners as well as an important trading venue for the nearby Indian pueblos. Later, when trains moved aside for automobiles, the famous Route 66 ran right through, making Gallup a well-known stop on the road to California.

Today the town is renowned for its turquoise and silver jewelry. In fact, about 80 percent of all such Southwestern adornments sold in the United States come from Gallup. A drive along Route 66 reveals numerous pawn shops and retail stores that sell the famous turquoise fashioned into glorious necklaces and modest hair barrettes, intricately tooled silver watchbands, and silver studs for the tips of your cowboy shirt's collar. Don't be afraid to go into pawnshops. They're open for business and are a time-honored way to shop in the Southwest.

Because the town is sandwiched between the huge Navajo reservation and the Zuñi pueblo, shops in the downtown area along East and West Coal Avenue offer a wide selection of beautifully crafted rugs, pottery, fetishes, kachina dolls, and sand paintings at fair prices. The following have been around a long time:

- **Richardson's Cash Pawn.** 222 West Highway 66; (505) 722–4762
- **Gilbert Ortega's Museum Quality Indian Jewelry.** 3306 East Highway 66; (505) 722–6666
- **Ellis Tanner's Trading Company.** 1980 State Highway 602; (505) 863–4434

El Rancho Hotel (all ages) 🏛 🚫 🍴
1000 East Highway 66; (505) 863–9311 or (800) 543–6351; www.elranchohotel.com.

This is an amazing place that both you and your kids will find delightful. Built in 1937 by the brother of silent movie mogul D. W. Griffith, it drew the rich and famous of Hollywood. While those hundreds of old-fashioned cowboy movies were made out in the deserts and mesas surrounding Gallup, the actors would stay at the hotel during the filming. There are some great publicity photos of a glamorous Katharine Hepburn, a rugged Kirk Douglas, and a boyish Ronald Reagan. Look around and try to find some of your favorites—and even your kids' favorites, because they still make movies out here. Then search out the silver dollars embedded in the counter of the reception desk in the main hall and take a look at the huge buffalo head looming from the robust wraparound balcony.

The Continental **Divide,**

roughly the ridge of the Rockies separating the streams that flow west (to the Pacific) from those that flow east (to the Atlantic), runs through much of northwestern New Mexico.

Gallup Cultural Center (ages 10 to 12)

201 East Highway 66; (505) 863–4131. Open Memorial Day to Labor Day, Monday through Saturday 9:00 A.M. to 4:00 P.M.; the rest of the year, closed Saturday. Admission: Free.

Located in a historic, renovated railroad station on Route 66, this project of the Southwest Indian Foundation includes the Kiva Cinema, showing documentaries of the area, and the Storyteller Museum, which features exhibits and in-depth interviews with experts in various fields, including weaving, sandpainting, Route 66, and silversmithing. There is also a cafe that offers espresso drinks, sandwiches, and burritos.

Playground of Dreams (all ages)

Located on the north side of I–40 on Maloney.

This playground is a great place for the kids to play and blow off steam. The park includes picnic tables and restrooms.

Red Rock Park and Museum (all ages)

300 West Historic 66 at Third Street in Gallup; (505) 863–1337. Open Monday through Saturday 8:00 A.M. to 4:30 P.M.; in the winter, closed Saturday. Admission: Free. Camping is $10.00 ($8.00 extra for hookups); the "horse hotel" is $10.00.

The red stone cliffs in this 640-acre park (off I–40), born in the Mesozoic era more than 200 million years ago, offer some spectacular scenery and walking trails. The museum (in Gallup) has well-displayed exhibits detailing the lives of the prehistoric Anasazi tribes, as well as the modern-day Suñi, Navajo, and Hopi, that your children will enjoy seeing. The park also has campgrounds, with showers, restrooms, and Internet access.

Nearby **Lake**

Ramah Lake. 42 miles southeast of Gallup on Highway 53; (505) 841–8881. The park has picnic areas, a boat ramp, and good trout and bass fishing.

Zuñi Pueblo (all ages)

Highway 602 to Highway 53; (505) 782–4481. Tribal Fish and Wildlife Department: (505) 782–5851 (for permit and information on conditions).

By far the jewel of the area, the pueblo is New Mexico's largest, with a population of 9,000. The legendary Seven Cities of Cibola were really the original Zuñi pueblos that the explorer Coronado conquered in his quest to find gold. These were abandoned during the Pueblo Revolt of 1680, and the present site was resettled in 1699 during the "reconquest." The great Zuñi annual winter festival is Shalako Day, a stunning nighttime ceremonial that features six messenger gods called the Shalako. They stand 10 feet tall and represent the six Zuñi kivas—holy underground worship spaces—which themselves represent the sacred directions: heaven, earth, and the four points of the compass. No photography, sketching, or sound recordings are allowed during this holy ritual, but once seen, you and your family will understand the unforgettable power and beauty of Native American spirituality. The dances take place in late November or early December (depending on when the tribal elders decide to set the festival date). The pueblo has many jewelry and pottery shops and an arts and crafts information center. With permits you can also camp on pueblo lands and fish and hunt in season.

A'shiwi A'wan Museum and Heritage Center (ages 10 to 12)

1222 Highway 53 in Zuñi; (505) 782–4403. Open Monday through Friday 9:00 A.M. to 5:30 P.M. Admission: $7.00 for adults, $5.00 for seniors 55 and over, $3.50 for children age 5 to 16.

This community-directed eco-museum is managed in harmony with the cultural and environmental values of the A'shiwi/Zuñi people. The center includes the A'shiwi Heritage Collection of prehistoric, historic, and contemporary objects, photographs, and information.

Nuestra Señora de Guadalupe (ages 10 to 12)

Inquire at St. Anthony's rectory (next door) for tours.

This charming, spare, early mission church is in the center of the old Zuñi village. Originally established in the mid-seventeenth century by the conquering Spanish, it was destroyed during the Pueblo Revolt of 1680, then rebuilt with the Spanish reoccupation in the 1690s. Since then the Zuñis and the Catholic Church seem to have compromised with

For Further Reference

Check out Tony Hillerman's *Dance Hall of the Dead* (Harper Collins) in which the Shalako Dance event is described.

one another, adding to the richness of both cultures. While over the next century and a half the building again fell into disrepair, a huge restoration in the late 1960s brought the building back to its former glory. Inside the church, the Zuñi artist Alex Seowtewa has painted on the 8-foot-thick walls the twenty-four large kachina images of the Zuñi culture. Tours of the building are given on Saturday.

Annual **Community Events**

MEMORIAL DAY TO LABOR DAY
Nightly Indian Dances and Market. Just east of the Gallup Cultural Center; (505) 722–2228. Sponsored by the city of Gallup, the dances and market begin every evening at 7:00 P.M.

THIRD WEEKEND IN JUNE
Western Jubilee Week. Red Rock State Park (parade held downtown first). One of the best rodeos in the area, it includes a special kids' rodeo, good country music, Indian dances, and a contest to pick this year's rodeo queen.

MID-AUGUST
Intertribal Indian Ceremonial. Red Rock State Park; (888) 685–2564. Admission: $6.00 per person; additional fees for performances, rodeo, and parking. Will Rogers once called this "The Greatest American Show," and it plays every year to thousands. This oldest all-Indian celebration, started in 1922, includes a rodeo, nightly dances, and a huge marketplace, where artists and craftspeople from the United States, Mexico, and Canada demonstrate their talents in basketry, pottery, silversmithing, beadwork, and leatherwork. There is also a rodeo, a parade, and a powwow. It is a wonderful way for children to experience and understand modern Native traditions and arts.

FIRST WEEKEND IN DECEMBER
Red Rock Balloon Rally. Red Rock State Park; (505) 722–9031 or (505) 863–0262. Between 150 and 200 balloonists participate in this annual event.

Where to Eat

El Rancho Restaurant. 1000 East Highway 66; (505) 863–9311. Good down-home meals at down-home prices. Open 6:30 A.M. to 10:00 P.M. daily. $–$$

Genaro's Cafe. 600 West Hill Avenue; (505) 863–6761. Good Mexican food. Open 10:00 A.M. to 8:00 P.M. Tuesday through Saturday. $$

Grampa's Grill. 2001 East Aztec; (505) 863–2151. Burgers are made individually and fresh to your specifications; they also have the most delicious salsa around. Open 8:00 A.M. to 8:30 P.M. daily. $$

Kristy's Coffee Shop. 1310 East U.S. Highway 66; (505) 863–4742. One of the many good, inexpensive restaurants that dot the town. Open twenty-four hours a day, seven days a week. $–$$

Virjie's. 2720 West Highway 66; (505) 863–5152. Try a great, bounteous breakfast burrito or some huevos rancheros here. Open 7:00 A.M. to 10:30 P.M. Monday through Saturday. $$

Where to Stay

El Rancho Hotel. 1000 East Highway 66; (505) 863–9311. Should you decide to stay the night, it'll be a challenge to pick a room. The reasonably priced lodgings are named for famous actors and actresses: Ida Lupino, Burt Lancaster, Loretta Young; for those seeking the grand experience, there's the Ronald Reagan presidential suite. $$

The Inn Best Western. 3009 West Highway 66; (505) 722–2221 or (800) 722–6399. The inn offers 124 rooms. $$

Redwood Lodge. 907 East Highway 66; (505) 863–5411. The lodge has fifteen rooms. $$

USA RV Park. I–40 at exit 16, west of town on Highway 66; (505) 863–5021. Here you'll find 100 sites with full hookups, fifteen tent sites, Kamping Kabins, playground, pool, and more. $

Zuñi Mountain Lodge Bed and Breakfast. 13 miles south of Thoreau (pronounced "threw"), east of Gallup (I–40 and NM 612); (505) 862–7769. Advance reservations required. $–$$

Four-Alarm **Alert**

With all the New Mexican food you may be trying for the first time, you'll probably encounter a four-alarm chile pepper without knowing it until it's too late. What to do? When both your nose and eyes begin to water, grab a glass of milk and a piece of bread if you can; these are the best "extinguishers." Next best are peanut butter, olive oil, yogurt, or those fruity pancake syrups. Ask the waitperson which chile (red or green) is hottest that day, and if you don't want to go straight with either, ask for "Christmas."

Code **Talkers**

If you get a chance, check out the **Navajo Code Talkers Room** in the Chamber of Commerce building (see address below). Through rare photos and memorabilia, you can learn about the Navajos' invaluable contribution to World War II, when the Navajo language was used to encode information. The 2002 film, *Wind Talkers*, starring Nicolas Cage and Adam Beach, was based on this fascinating history. For hours, call (505) 722–2228.

For More Information

Chamber of Commerce. Next to Amtrak Station at 103 West Highway 66; (505) 722–2228; www.gallupchamber.com. (Pick up the *Indian Trader,* a monthly about the goings-on in Gallup, and maps to a self-guided walking or driving tour.)

Visitor's Bureau. 201 East Highway 66; (505) 863–3841 or (800) 242–4282; www.gallupnm.org.

Grants

I–40 at exit 85, about an hour west of Albuquerque.

The town of Grants is modest but interesting. It began as a homestead on the trail west. The man who owned it, Don Diego Antonio Chavez, also controlled the only spring and charged a dime to use it. Then, three brothers by the name of Grant got a contract to lay railroad track as far as the area near the old farm. Soon people started calling the area Grant's Station, but it finally became just Grants. The town has had a long and prosperous life, first as a railroad depot, then as a logging center, and finally as a uranium boom town. The Navajo call the area Turquoise Hill because, in the Navajo legend, First Woman scattered turquoise here after she fastened the mountain to the earth with a knife.

New Mexico Museum of Mining (ages 10 to 12)
100 North Iron Avenue; (505) 287–4802 or (800) 748–2142. Open Monday through Saturday 9:00 A.M. to 4:00 P.M. Admission: $3.00 for adults, $2.00 for seniors and kids 7–18, free for kids 6 and under.

Grants was considered the uranium capital of the United States before the mines ran out in the 1970s. The museum is built right over an old mine. You and the kids get to go down into the once working mine in a genuine mine elevator. You'll see firsthand all the tremendous machinery and the equipment once used in this modern-day operation that turned "yellowcake" into the uranium that ended up in atomic bombs and power plants. Individual and family tours are usually self-guided, but there are many guides around who are former miners and will happily answer questions as you explore the tunnels. Check out the sculpture made out of old drill bits in front of the museum.

El Morro National Monument and Inscription Rock (ages 10 to 12)

I–40 and Highway 53; 43 miles southwest of Grants; (505) 783–4226; www.nps.gov/elmo. Visitor center open daily 9:00 A.M. to 5:00 P.M. Trails close an hour earlier. Admission: $3.00 for adults, free for kids 17 and under, $5.00 per campsite (nine sites available).

The route to El Morro is one of the loveliest drives in the northwest area. El Morro (Spanish for "headlands" or "bluffs") is the oldest national monument in the United States and is a lesson in history. Because of its warm, pleasant location next to a pool of good, clear water, these headlands served as a kind of ancient campground for passing caravans of Native Americans, Spanish conquistadors, and anyone else who thought to take a break from the long trek west. Inscription Rock, where travelers left their names, thoughts, dates, even designs, serves as a 200-foot history book of the Southwest. Before there were Pilgrims at Plymouth Rock, there was the Spanish explorer Don Juan de Oñate, who left his name at El Morro and a little note about why he was passing through—it's dated 1605. It will be an important history experience for your children to enjoy. There is a visitor center (pick up a trail guide there; it will tell you about each inscription) and paved trails to all the sights. There is a nine-space camping area near the monument. It has water but little else.

El Malpais National Monument (ages 10 to 12)
I–40 and Highway 117 or Highway 53 (10 miles south of Grants); (505) 285–4641; www.nm.blm.gov. You can get maps at two locations: the Park Service Center, located on Highway 53, (505) 783–4774, is open 8:00 A.M. to dusk every day; or the Northwest New Mexico Visitor Center, 1900 East Santa Fe Avenue, (505) 876–2783.

The name of this 20,000-acre wilderness area comes from the Spanish word for "badlands," but the Navajo have a claim on it, too. One of their great stories explains that the black lava rocks dominating the landscape came about when twin war gods killed off the giant who lived on top of Mount Taylor. They cut off his head. The blood flowed out black and covered the land. When it dried, the results are what you see as you drive through. Full of volcanoes, forests, sandstone canyons, lava flows, and caves, it is a wondrous spot for the kids. The craggy terrain invites hikers to explore, but driving through can be almost as rewarding. Go to the visitor center first for detailed maps and information.

From here, stay on Highway 117 and you'll proceed through the **Narrows,** where the road tightens. On either side huge sandstone cliffs and large chunks of lava squeeze you through the pass. If you want to explore more, drive across County Road 42 (not for motor coaches, though). It will take you to the west area of El Malpais and the **Chain of Craters.** There are also the wind- and water-sculpted **La Ventana Natural Arch,** the **Sandstone Bluffs Overlook,** and the **Laval Tubes,** formed by hot lava. The tubes are about 17 miles long, and you can drive through them (10 miles or so off Highway 53). Check with the Visitor Information Center in Grants first to get a feel for what might suit your family. You can pick up maps and a list of hikes and activities in the area. No matter where you explore in El Malpais National Monument, be aware that the lava terrain is unstable and sharp in places. Wear athletic shoes or hiking boots—no sandals!

Annual **Community Events**

FOURTH OF JULY WEEKEND
Wild West Days and Fireworks; Parade and Grants Rodeo and Jamboree; Arts and Crafts Show. (800) 748–2142

FIRST WEEKEND IN OCTOBER
Great Fall Chile Fiesta. (505) 287–4802. Festivities include chile and salsa cook-offs.

Bandera Volcano/Ice Caves (ages 10 to 12)

Off Highway 53 about 25 miles southwest of Grants; (888) 423–2283; www.icecaves.com. Open 8:00 A.M. to one hour before sunset. Admission: $8.00 for adults, $4.00 for children over 5, $6.50 for seniors.

After driving around these desert regions, you may come to believe that New Mexico is one big, flat, hot platter. But you'd be wrong. Directly under El Malpais is a huge glacier! No matter how hot it gets on top, down below, it's never above freezing. To make things even more mysterious, not too far away are the remains of a volcano. The site is on privately owned property that the National Park Service is negotiating to buy. After you pay the entrance fee, walk the volcano path (about ¾ mile) to the caldera (cauldron), where you can get a wonderful look down into the "after" picture of a volcanic eruption. After you imagine just how hot it had to be when it blew, cool yourselves down by visiting the ice caves some 300 yards away. Some of the laval tubes of El Malpais collapsed when they cooled and provided a perfect setting for water that flowed in later and froze.

Bluewater Lake State Park (all ages)

I–40 and Highway 412 (28 miles west of Grants); (505) 876–2391. Open year-round. Between May 15 and September 1, be sure to make a reservation (www.nmparks.com). Admission: $5.00 per car, $10.00 for overnight camping ($4.00 extra with hookups). Showers and a dumpsite are available.

Bluewater Lake is a very large body of water some 7,400 feet above sea level. In fact, the lake takes up about half of the park, measuring 2,300 acres in this 5,000-acre park. In the summer, there's catfish and trout fishing. In the winter, the lake freezes *hard*, so if your family is into ice-fishing, this is the place to do it. There are also marinas, a cafe, and a shop with lots of fishing supplies.

Some Movies Made in New Mexico

The Ballad of Gregorio Cortez (1981)
Butch Cassidy and the Sundance Kid (1968)
Chisum (1969)
City Slickers (1991)
Easy Rider (1968)
Lonesome Dove (1989)
Oklahoma (1954)
Superman (1978)

Where to Eat

As with most good-size towns, Grants has the usual fast food places, but there are also some local-flavored restaurants.

De Mautry's Sandwich Shop. 907 North First Street; (505) 285–4550. Sandwiches and casual fare. Open Monday through Friday 11:00 A.M. to 8:00 P.M., Saturday to 3:00 P.M. $–$$

El Cafecito. 820 East Santa Fe Avenue; (505) 285–6229. Homey New Mexican dishes. Open Monday through Saturday 7:00 A.M. to 9:00 P.M. $–$$

Monte Carlo. 721 West Santa Fe Avenue; (505) 287–9250. Historic landmark restaurant in old adobe building. Good steaks and Mexican food. Children's menu. Open daily 7:00 A.M. to 10:00 P.M. $–$$

Tres Maria Bakery. 801 East High Street; (505) 287–7602. Wonderful baked goods and sandwiches. Open Monday through Saturday 6:00 A.M. to 5:30 P.M. $–$$

Where to Stay

Grants has two dozen motels and several campgrounds; most are located on Santa Fe Avenue.

Best Western Inn. 1501 East Santa Fe Avenue; (505) 287–7901 or (800) 528–1234; www.bestwestern.com. The inn has 126 rooms. $$

Desert Sun Motel. 1121 East Santa Fe Avenue; (505) 287–7925. The motel has eighteen rooms. $

Grants/Cibola Sands RV Park. Highway 53 south of Grants; (505) 287–4376. The forty-six sites have full hookups; small grocery store. $

Lavaland RV Campground. 1901 East Santa Fe Avenue; (505) 287–8665. $

For More Information

Chamber of Commerce/Visitor Bureau. 100 North Iron Avenue; (505) 287–4802 or (800) 748–2142; www.grants.org.

Northwest New Mexico Visitor Center. 1900 East Santa Fe Avenue; (505) 876–2783.

Acoma Pueblo

I–40 at exit 96, between Laguna Pueblo and Grants; (505) 552–6604; www.puebloof
acoma.org.

The Acoma Pueblo will be memorable for both you and your children. It's advertised on
billboards everywhere as **Sky City** because it sits on the 387-foot-high Sky City Mesa. Sky
City is considered one of the oldest continuously inhabited places in North America. The
Acoma (whose name means "People of the White Rock") have lived here for hundreds of
years. A few families continue to reside here. Property is passed from the parents to the
youngest daughter of the family. In exchange, she must care for the parents until their
death before she becomes the new owner. Once the only way up to the pueblo was via a
system of ladders. Then in 1920, Hollywood came calling. In order to make the movie *Red-
skin*, the film company built a road to the top; the Acoma have maintained it ever since.

No visitor is allowed on the mesa unaccompanied. You must register at the visitor center and buy a ticket for the guided bus tour. Tours run regularly from 8:00 A.M. to 6:00 P.M.
every half hour; (505) 470–4966. Admission: $10.00 for camera use (no videos or sketch-
ing). Tour fees: $8.00 for adults, $6.00 for children 6–17, $7.00 for seniors. The pueblo is
closed at various times during the year; call ahead.

Once at the top, the Acoma guide walks you through the sad and often brutal history
of the Spanish occupation. In the 1500s the Acoma, deeply resenting their conquerors,
killed ten Spanish soldiers by throwing them off the edge of the mesa. The Spanish
explorer Don Juan de Oñate retaliated by cutting off the right foot of every adult male and
selling all the children into slavery in exchange for the bell that still hangs in the tower of
the mission church. When you walk through the church's graveyard, you'll see an adobe
wall surrounding it. In the far wall there's a child-size hole that the Acoma made so that if
the children ever returned, they would be able to get in and find their parents. Have the
guide point out Enchanted Mesa and the valley between the mesas. Legend has it that
one day a sudden rainstorm trapped a mother and daughter on top of Enchanted Mesa.
Rather than remain there and starve, the two threw themselves off the edge. As you walk
through the narrow streets, consider that there is no electricity or running water. The
famous Acoma potters who live here have some of their wares on display and for sale.
Many pieces of this marvelously intricate, black-on-white pottery are in museums around
the country. If you can afford to invest in a piece, it would be worthwhile doing so. If you
wish to speak with some of the owners of the homes, the guide will invite you into the res-
idences where the pottery is sold.

KTNN **660**

If you would enjoy listening to Navajo radio, tune in to KTNN, 660 on the AM
dial.

Pueblo **Revolt**

The area east of the town of Grants is the site of the Pueblo Revolt. As the Spanish colony grew in the seventeenth century, the native people grew increasingly resentful of the poor treatment they received. They were often subjected to slavery and forced to adopt Christianity. A doctor from the Tewa tribe, called Pope, led a pueblo-wide rebellion on August 10, 1680, aided by the Apaches. Missions were destroyed, and priests and colonists were killed. The Spanish returned in 1692, though, and had reoccupied the area by the turn of the century. The Acoma were the last to concede.

Laguna Pueblo

Off I–40, 50 miles west of Albuquerque; (505) 552–6654.

This pueblo was established by refugees in the 1690s during the resettling of the area following the Pueblo Revolt. While it is not really a tourist venue, there's a charming mission church here worth seeing. The building is usually locked, but if you visit the church office around back, someone may be able to show you the interior. This is a prosperous pueblo because there was a rich vein of uranium for which the Laguna received royalties. The mine is tapped out now, but a large pueblo-owned electronics company is the major employer.

It's a peaceful locality, with quiet views across the desert. The noted contemporary author Leslie Marmon Silko was born here, and her acclaimed book, *Ceremony*, speaks of the many people she knew as she grew up on the pueblo.

Feast **Day**

The big Feast Day at the Laguna Pueblo is St. Joseph's, on September 19. (They also celebrate on March 19.) You may want to take the kids. Call (505) 552–6654 for information.

Shrine of **Los Portales**

Just north of the Laguna Pueblo off Highway 129 is the Laguna village of Cebolleta. Here you'll find the lovely Shrine of Los Portales, where the statue of Our Lady of Sorrows is enshrined in a natural cave. The spring water seeping through the walls of the cave is considered holy. The original statue brought with the Spanish conquerors is in the mission church in the village.

Glossary

Adobe: A building material composed of mud, clay, straw, and sometimes manure.

Atole: A thick, hot corn cereal.

Bizcochito: A crisp sugar cookie with a little anise thrown in.

Bosque (BOSS-kay): Forest, or riverbed vegetation.

Breakfast burrito: A warm flour tortilla usually wrapped around scrambled eggs, potatoes, bacon, cheese, and some green chile.

Burrito: A warm flour tortilla wrapped around refried beans, or meat and cheese.

Calabacitas: A vegetable dish of zucchini, corn, chile, and cheese.

Caldera: Ancient volcanic crater that now is usually a deep, broad, and grassy bowl.

Carne adovada: Pork marinated in red chile and baked.

Casita: Little house.

Cerro: Hill. *Cerrito* (little hill). *Cerrillos* (low hills).

Cerveza: Beer.

Chalupas: Fried corn tortilla filled with meat or refried beans, onion, cheese, lettuce, tomato, sour cream, and guacamole.

Enchilada: Similar to a burrito, but with a corn tortilla, and swimming in chile and cheese.

Farolitos: Also known as *luminarias*, these "small lanterns" are made from paper bags with a layer of sand at the bottom supporting votive candles. They are used during celebrations to line walkways, walls, or rooftops.

Fetish: A carved rock that resembles an animal and is used as a talisman for luck, protection, or prosperity.

Flan: A light custard with a syrup topping.

Frito pie: Corn chips smothered with beef, beans, chile, cheese, and onions.

Fry bread: Native American confection made from fried bread covered in confectioner's sugar and cinnamon.

Green chile stew: Soup made with green chile, pork or beef, tomatoes, and potatoes. Renowned remedy for a cold!

Guacamole: A side dish or condiment of chopped and mashed avocado to which onions, garlic, and tomatoes have been added.

Horno (OR-noh): An outdoor, beehive-shaped oven for baking bread.

Huevos rancheros: Corn tortillas under fried eggs, beans, chile, and cheese.

Kachina: Usually refers to the Hopi dolls that were made for the children to acquaint them with the gods. Can also mean spirit, the dancers that portray them, and thunder-heads.

Kiva: Originally, an underground ceremonial or meeting place, where there was felt to be a link to the womb of the earth; now also used to describe a traditional indoor corner fire-place.

Latillas (La-TEE-yas): These are small, twiglike branches that are sometimes placed between *vigas*.

Llano (YAN-oh): Plain.

Mesa: Table.

Molina: Mill.

Ojo (O-ho): Literally "eye," but it also means spring.

Pico de Gallo (PEE-ko deh GUY-yo): Literally, rooster's beak. A side dish made up of tomatoes, onions, jalapeños, and a dash of cilantro.

Posole (Po-SO-lay): Hominy cooked with green chile and chicken until it pops.

Powwow: A Native American celebration involving dancing, costumes, and plays.

Quesadilla (KAY-seh-DI-ya): Spanish toasted-cheese sandwich, made with a flour tortilla instead of bread.

Ristras: Decorative hanging strings of dried red chile pods, usually hung outside from exposed *vigas*.

Sand painting: Sand paintings were created by medicine men as a curative device and were destroyed deliberately after healing the sick.

Sipapu: The name for the hole in the floor of a kiva through which the spirits can pass between the two worlds.

Sopaipilla (So-pie-PEE-ya): Similar to fry bread, a fried pocket dough served as a side dish or dessert with honey (instead of sugar and cinnamon).

Tamale (Ta-MA-lay): Masa, or corn meal, cooked with chile and pork and steamed in a corn husk.

Viga: Full-size tree trunk supporting a house's roof or ceiling. Usually exposed (inside and out) and unpainted.

Index

About the Author

Kate Winslow is a writer and editor who made her home in Santa Fe for seven years before recently seeking grayer pastures in Brooklyn, New York. Her work has appeared in the *Santa Fe Reporter, Cowboys and Indians,* and *Food & Wine,* among other publications.